CAMBRIDGE LIBRARY COLLECTION

Books of enduring scholarly value

History

The books reissued in this series include accounts of historical events and movements by eye-witnesses and contemporaries, as well as landmark studies that assembled significant source materials or developed new historiographical methods. The series includes work in social, political and military history on a wide range of periods and regions, giving modern scholars ready access to influential publications of the past.

Merton College, Oxford

The oldest of all Oxford and Cambridge colleges, Merton College enjoys a distinguished past that reflects many of the most significant moments in British history, including the Black Death and the Civil War. These and other crucial events are explored with wit and insight in White's chronicle of the college, first published in 1906. A biblical scholar, White was made a fellow and lecturer in theology at Merton in 1895, where he stayed until his promotion to Dean of Christ Church in 1905. Even after his departure, he remained intrigued by the history and customs of his old college and was eager to share his knowledge outside the academic community. Worldly as well as scholarly, White always intended his volume to be accessible to a wide audience, describing it in his preface as a 'popular handbook' rather than a scholarly tome; a function it continues to fulfil today.

Cambridge University Press has long been a pioneer in the reissuing of out-of-print titles from its own backlist, producing digital reprints of books that are still sought after by scholars and students but could not be reprinted economically using traditional technology. The Cambridge Library Collection extends this activity to a wider range of books which are still of importance to researchers and professionals, either for the source material they contain, or as landmarks in the history of their academic discipline.

Drawing from the world-renowned collections in the Cambridge University Library, and guided by the advice of experts in each subject area, Cambridge University Press is using state-of-the-art scanning machines in its own Printing House to capture the content of each book selected for inclusion. The files are processed to give a consistently clear, crisp image, and the books finished to the high quality standard for which the Press is recognised around the world. The latest print-on-demand technology ensures that the books will remain available indefinitely, and that orders for single or multiple copies can quickly be supplied.

The Cambridge Library Collection will bring back to life books of enduring scholarly value (including out-of-copyright works originally issued by other publishers) across a wide range of disciplines in the humanities and social sciences and in science and technology.

Merton College, Oxford

Henry Julian White

CAMBRIDGE UNIVERSITY PRESS

Cambridge, New York, Melbourne, Madrid, Cape Town, Singapore,
São Paolo, Delhi, Dubai, Tokyo, Mexico City

Published in the United States of America by Cambridge University Press, New York

www.cambridge.org
Information on this title: www.cambridge.org/9781108017978

© in this compilation Cambridge University Press 2010

This edition first published 1906
This digitally printed version 2010

ISBN 978-1-108-01797-8 Paperback

The College

Monographs

THE COLLEGE
MONOGRAPHS
Edited and Illustrated by
EDMUND H. NEW

TRINITY COLLEGE,
CAMBRIDGE
        W. W. ROUSE BALL.

ST. JOHN'S COLLEGE,
CAMBRIDGE
        THE SENIOR BURSAR.

KING'S COLLEGE,
CAMBRIDGE
        C. R. FAY.

MAGDALEN COLLEGE,
OXFORD
        THE PRESIDENT.

NEW COLLEGE,
OXFORD
        A. O. PRICKARD.

MERTON COLLEGE,
OXFORD
        REV. H. J. WHITE.

W M
"Mob
Quad"

E.H.N   1906

MERTON ⬡ COLLEGE

OXFORD

BY

H. J. WHITE, M.A.

FORMERLY FELLOW AND CHAPLAIN OF
MERTON COLLEGE

ILLUSTRATED BY

EDMUND H. NEW

1906: LONDON   J. M. DENT & CO.
NEW YORK: E. P. DUTTON & CO.

PREFACE

THE following pages are intended to furnish a short and popular handbook to Merton College. The alterations of the last few years have changed its outward appearance considerably, and may therefore make such a book of use even to those who possess the larger college history of Mr. Henderson.[1] To that book and to the late Warden's *Memorials of Merton* I owe more than I can easily tell; had it not been for the information so patiently accumulated and so pleasantly imparted in them, I could never have ventured on this smaller undertaking, and I must especially thank Mr. Henderson and his publisher for permitting

[1] "Merton College" in *Oxford University College Histories.* London: F. E. Robinson, 1899 (now published by Hutchinson & Co.).

vii

PREFACE

me to quote from his book. My only justification for making such extensive use of other men's labours lies in the hope that this handbook may induce many readers to study those labours for themselves.

I must also thank the Warden for much kind advice and information.

H. J. White.

March 1906.

CONTENTS

CHAPTER I

WALTER OF MERTON AND THE ESTABLISHMENT OF THE COLLEGIATE SYSTEM

CHAPTER II

THE COLLEGE BUILDINGS

ix

CONTENTS

CHAPTER III

THE COLLEGE LIFE AND HISTORY

CONTENTS

CHAPTER IV

NOTABLE MEMBERS OF MERTON COLLEGE

LIST OF ILLUSTRATIONS

The
Library

E.H.N.   1906

Merton College

CHAPTER I

WALTER OF MERTON AND THE ESTABLISH MENT OF THE COLLEGIATE SYSTEM

THE first thing to be impressed upon all visitors to Merton College, is that it is the oldest in either Oxford or Cambridge; it is also a year older than the English Parliament. The first regular Parliament was summoned in 1265, and Merton College was founded in 1264. It is true that two other colleges, University and Balliol, are placed before Merton in the University Calendar, and claim to be older; and as benefactions for the support of poor students in Oxford they are. William of Durham left in 1249 a sum of money (310 marks) to maintain a number of Masters in the Schools of Oxford; but this was not much more than a pension fund to be administered by the University, and though some loans to scholars were made in 1253 and the following years, the first four Masters who were to be regular recipients of the fund were not selected till 1280. They were then formed into a corporate

A

community, granted a code of Statutes, and
"after the pattern of the nephews and
scholars of Walter de Merton they were
gathered under a single roof."[1] Similarly
with Balliol College; between the years
1260 and 1269 John de Balliol gave money
for the support of poor scholars at Oxford
in a hired house; but there was no sort of
organisation in the scheme till 1282, when
his widow Devorguilla drew up a code of
Statutes constituting a corporate community,
but even then without complete self-govern-
ment, which was not obtained for many
years.

As gifts of money, therefore, for the support of what we should now call "un-
attached students" at Oxford both University and Balliol Colleges may claim to
be earlier than Merton; but as a College
in our sense of the word, that is as a
corporate community governing itself, pos-
sessing estates in the country and its
group of buildings in Oxford, housing its
members within its walls, providing in-
struction for them and exercising discipline
over them, Merton is sixteen years older
than University College, and eighteen years
older than Balliol. And Merton gave the
example not only to Oxford but to Cambridge; the system of life established by
our Founder was copied quickly at the sister
University; and when Hugh de Balsham,

[1] F. C. Conybeare on "University College," quoted
in Henderson, p. 285.

Bishop of Ely, founded the College of Peterhouse in 1280, he commanded that his scholars should live according to the rule of the scholars at Oxford who are called "of Merton." Twenty years, therefore, in the latter part of the thirteenth century—from 1264 to 1284—saw the establishment of the College system in both Universities, a system which after six hundred years of life is as strong and valuable as ever; and for this we have to thank Walter de Merton.

Previous to that time the students who were not already members of the religious orders lived in private lodgings or small licensed halls, and the only sort of discipline exercised over them was that of the two Proctors. The city of Oxford in the thirteenth century has been described by the late Warden of Merton, Mr. Brodrick,[1] as "not diversified by picturesque cloisters and quadrangles, or embowered in peaceful gardens, but encircled with a loopholed wall, crowded with dingy hostelries, intersected by a labyrinth of squalid lanes, and swarming with a mixed multitude of priests and vagrants." But that is only one side of the picture; those narrow streets had buildings gorgeous as well as squalid; and in Castle, Abbey, and Church with their inmates, in processions military or religious, in general dress and decoration, there must have been a picturesqueness of form and a richness of colour far beyond anything

[1] *Memorials of Merton College*, p. 3.

3

that Oxford can show now. Yet the
social position of the students and their
manners were very different from those of
the modern undergraduate; most of the
students were poor, lived roughly, and fought
hard; they had frequent brawls with the
townsmen and with each other. The very
year 1264 saw the return to Oxford, under
Simon de Montfort's safe-conduct, of a considerable body of students who had migrated
to Northampton the previous year in consequence of a riot; while the institution
of the office of Proctors, much about the
same time,[1] was mainly for the purpose of
keeping the peace among the scholars, and
especially between those from the North of
England and those from the South, or the
Northern and Southern "nations" as they
were called. It was doubtless the experi-
ence of the evils of University life under
these conditions which led Walter de
Merton to devise a scheme somewhat
similar to that already prevailing at Paris,
by which a number of students could be
gathered together and live a collegiate
life.

Walter de Merton was born in the early
part of the thirteenth century, though the
exact year is unknown; nor is it certain,
though it is probable enough, that he was
born at Merton in Surrey and received his

<hr/>

[1] The first Proctors in the official list are set down
as officiating in 1267: see Brodrick, *History of the
University of Oxford*, p. 40.

education at the Priory there.[1]   He appears
to have come up to Oxford afterwards to
complete his studies, and to have been an
inmate of Mauger Hall, now the Cross
Inn, in the Cornmarket.   He was in Holy
Orders probably as early as 1238, and seems
to have soon won favour with King Henry
III. ; in 1258 he was chancellor, and again
in 1260 ; removed by the barons in the
same year, he was restored in the next by
the King ; and during the troubled time
after that year Henry while absent in
France seems to have left the management of the kingdom largely in his hands.
In 1264 the barons gained the upper hand
and Walter of Merton resigned the chan-
cellorship ; and the leisure he now enjoyed
gave him the power of perfecting a scheme
he had been considering for some years, for
the foundation of a house in his manor of
Malden in Surrey, but in connection with
the University of Oxford.

This house at Malden was not to be a
college for study, but an institution of
" scholares de Merton " as they were called,
who should live under the supervision of a
Warden and bailiffs, with two or three
chaplains, for the purpose of managing the

[1] Students should avoid confusing Merton College
at Oxford with Merton Priory at Merton ; in the
" Essay on the History of English Gothic Church
Architecture " by G. Gilbert Scott, 1881, we are
gravely informed that Thomas à Becket was educated
at Merton College, Oxford (p. 136)—more than a
century before the College existed.

Surrey estates which the Founder had made over to them ; and these were to support a body of twenty students living at Oxford, or if advisable at some other place where the *studium generale* flourished. Thus the original foundation was double ; a house

THE COLLEGE FROM THE MEADOWS

of students at Oxford, and a house of estate-managers at Malden ; but the latter existed to support the former, and were subject to an annual visitation from them for inquiry into their management of the goods committed to their charge.

The next few years saw the Founder acquiring land in Oxford. The entire site

of the present College buildings, with the
exception of the Fellows' garden and the
ground occupied by St. Alban Hall,[1] was
his by 1268; he obtained it by the pur-
chase of one house from the Prior of St.
Frideswide's, and another from a London
Jew named Jacob, and by enclosing under
royal charter a large piece of vacant ground
near the City wall; while for the site of
the College Chapel he obtained permission
to pull down the already existing Church
of St. John the Baptist. This church and
the right to present to it were formally
made over to the College by the Abbot of
Reading Abbey on condition that the new
Chapel should also serve as the Church for
the parish of St. John the Baptist; and this
it did till the year 1891, when the parish
was united with that of St. Peter's in the
East, a living which had also been acquired
for the College by Walter of Merton.

During the years following 1264, gifts
of money and land and the patronage of
several livings were made over to the new
foundation, and in 1270 it became advisable to modify the first Statutes of the
College. The number of scholars was
increased, their lines of study more carefully marked out, and their discipline made
more strict; one in twenty was called a
Vicenarius and was to act as monitor; and
a Sub-Warden was to rule over the whole
society in Oxford.

1 For St. Alban Hall, see below, pp. 20, 29, 75.

Four years later came the last revision, for many centuries, of the Statutes. During the ten years 1264–74 much property had been acquired for the College in various parts of England besides Surrey; it was obvious, therefore, that the estates could be as well administered from Oxford as from Malden, while it would be far better to have all the members concentrated in one place; and so in 1274 the whole of the Malden establishment was moved up to Oxford, with the exception of a few brethren, probably farm bailiffs. It was in 1274, then, that Merton College took the form it has preserved ever since, and it may be worth while giving a short account of the Statutes which moulded it.

The members were called "scholares," *scholars*; there was no distinction between "scholars" and "Fellows" as the terms are used now, for the "scholares" were junior Fellows,[1] and after a year's probation would be elected for life, or so long as the Warden and other scholars should approve of their conduct and diligence. Any scholar who gained a wealthy benefice, or left the House and gave up study; or became a monk, was to lose his scholarship; this last provision is important as showing Walter of Merton's intention of making his College a foundation for encouraging learning amongst the secular

[1] The scholars are called Fellows ("Socii") as early as 1284; see *Memorials of Merton*, p. 25 *note*.

clergy as distinct from the religious orders. He was raising up a rival to the monastic system which had absorbed so much of the learning and devotion of the age, and at the same time he was copying much of the monastic life and organisation.

None were to be admitted to the College save such persons as were of thoroughly good character, in need of assistance, of ability for study, and desirous of improvement. Beyond this, nothing is said as to an "entrance examination"; but they were to have the year's probation above mentioned before they were finally admitted into the body. In electing scholars, preference was to be given first to the Founder's kin, and then to candidates from the diocese of Winchester and other dioceses and places in which the College estates were situated.

The number of scholars was to be regulated by the state of the College revenues, and each was to receive fifty shillings a year, out of which they were to pay for their commons; this seems extremely small, but when we remember that the College Library and its fittings cost a little over £450, and the Chapel Tower apparently under £186, it becomes clear that money went a great deal further then. The scholars were to have a common table, and as far as possible a common dress; one was to read at meals, and the rest were to listen in silence; in their rooms they were to abstain from noise and interruption of

9

their fellows, and to apply themselves with all diligence to study; when they spoke it was to be in Latin; they were not to introduce strangers, even near relatives, lest the quiet of their companions should be disturbed. To every twenty men, or ten should such further division be necessary (and apparently it was), was to be appointed a monitor to guide their studies and keep discipline; the *Vicenarius* became a *Decanus* or Dean, and the number of Deans in Merton, for there were three until 1858, very likely corresponded to the average number of members (thirty) of the College in early times. In addition to the Deans there was to be one person in every chamber, where scholars were resident, of more mature age than the rest, who was to have superintendence over them — a provision which shows that in those days it was customary for several scholars to share one room.

The Warden was to exercise a general superintendence over all the officers and members of the House; his election was partly in the hands of the seven senior scholars, partly in those of the Visitor,[1] the latter having to appoint one out of three candidates selected by the former. The appointment of other officers, Sub-Warden, Chaplains, and Bursars, was to lie in the hands of the Warden; there were careful provisions for seeing that the College estates

[1] For the office of Visitor, see below, p. 64.

were properly managed, and its revenues
wisely administered, for pensioning the
members in old age or sickness, and for
expelling them when unworthy; and they
were all exhorted "in God's name and by
their hopes of happiness both in this life
and in the next, that in all things and
above all things they ever observe unity
and mutual charity, peace, concord, and
love."

Walter of Merton ordained that at the
"Scrutinies" or College Meetings as we
should call them, when the whole business
of the College was to be examined into,
Divine Service was to be solemnly per-
formed for the Founder and other benefactors, living or dead; and the Statutes
were to be read in the presence of the
whole College, "with a view to the preservation and everlasting remembrance of
this Charity."

The Latin versicles, responses, and
prayer, which are said daily in the College
Chapel after every service, and the English
"Founder's prayers" said on certain days
in the year, date from a later age. They
form part of an occasional service, "Com-
memoratio Benefactorum," in the Elizabethan Latin Prayer Book of 1560; the
full Commemoration Service in English was
published ten years later.[1]

Walter of Merton did not live to see

---

[1] Procter and Frere, *New History of the Book of
Common Prayer*, p. 122 f.

many years of his new foundation. On 27th October 1277 he died from the effects of a fall from his horse, when crossing a river, probably the Medway; it is uncertain whether he was drowned, or succumbed to the shock and chill. Fortunately for the College he had only the day before added a codicil to his will, devising to it the whole residue of his personalty instead of a fixed sum of £1000. Till about fifty years ago the College bell was tolled every Friday at 10.30 A.M., the day and hour on which the Founder was supposed to have met his death.

Of his personal appearance we can form a good guess. The portrait in the Hall is a fancy one, but the corbel in the Chapel on the north side of the east window (a plaster cast of which is in the Common Room) shows us a strong, heavy, stout face, suggestive of a good deal of power; while the measurements taken of his bones when his coffin in Rochester Cathedral was opened in 1852 proved that he must have been a big man, well over six feet in height. The full length statue over the College gate is probably, as regards its face, a copy from the window corbel; and the kneeling figure in the lower carved slab may have been also taken from the same source. He was worthy of commemoration not only in Merton but all over England; for he founded a system of education which combined the intellectual and social sides in a peculiarly happy way, and which has influenced the national character quite as much as, if not more than, our public schools have done ; the founder of one College in fact, he was the founder of them all in design.

CHAPTER II

THE COLLEGE BUILDINGS

THE visitor who approaches Merton
from Christ Church or by Grove
Street will first be struck by the Chapel
with its magnificent choir, transepts, and
tower, and then proceeding east will see a
fairly long line of buildings facing the
street. This is the north side of the
Front Quad, extending now without any
break into St. Alban Hall, from which it
used to be divided by the front door and
entrance Hall of the Warden's House.
The lines of the front door are clearly
visible though the lower part of it has
been walled up, and the upper part converted into a window. Towards the west
end is the College porch with a tower over
it. This is the most interesting part of the
buildings as viewed from the street, and
was built by Warden Rodeborne (or Rudborn) in 1418 ; the statues above the gate
represent Henry III. (*l.*) and the Founder
(*r.*) ; the face of the Founder was probably
copied from that on the corbel to the east
window of the chapel. The curious piece
of symbolical sculpture now immediately over
the door originally stood much higher, and

14

*The College Chapel
from Merton St*

can be seen in that position not only in Loggan's print (1675) but in the Oxford Almanack engraving of 1772; it was brought down to its present position during the restoration of 1836–38, a doubtful advantage; for though it can be seen more clearly it can also be touched by careless or adventurous hands, and one of the sculptured animals lost its head as recently as 1897, though it has since been supplied with a new one.

This carving is referred to by Antony Wood as "that elegant effigies of St. John Πρυδόμου preaching in the wildernesse cut in stone over Merton College gate" (*City of Oxford*, i. p. 175); and John Pointer in his *Oxoniensis Academia*, published 1749, describes it thus: "You find the Baptist (our Saviour's Fore-runner) in the Habit of a Monk; and our Saviour himself coming after him, with the Dove over his Head. . . . There is likewise the *Agnus Dei*, and Sun of Righteousness, with the New Testament in his Hand, bringing a new Revelation to the World. Also the Serpent condemn'd to creep on the Ground, whose Head 'twas prophesy'd our Saviour should break. Likewise the Unicorn, whose Horn was an Emblem of our Saviour's Exaltation. You may observe likewise the Palm-trees, with Branches broken off to strow on the Ground, in his Procession to Jerusalem. And over all, the Pelican feeding her young ones with her own Blood."

Pointer repeats the current tradition that the sculpture belonged to the old Church of St. John the Baptist ; but it certainly gives the impression of being a fifteenth rather

THE COLLEGE GATE

than a thirteenth or twelfth century piece of work, and we feel inclined to assign it to the same date as the two statues. And Pointer's explanation of the symbols is

18

incorrect ; the kneeling figure is a Bishop, not a Monk, and is obviously intended for the Founder ; and the figure standing behind is the Baptist, not the Saviour. The great book is the book with the seven seals, with the Lamb on one side, the Unicorn on the other, and the Lion behind. The other animals and the trees probably have no special signification but are simply the conventional background and foreground with which the mediæval sculptors and artists loved to adorn their work.

The tower over the main gateway very possibly formed the Warden's lodgings at first ;[1] this was in old times the natural residence for the Head of a House, though at the present day it has survived only in New College. The staircase west of the Tower was rebuilt in 1631, and the front eastwards in 1588–91 ; the street front was partially altered in 1812, and wholly remodelled in the restoration of 1836–38. These alterations have made it the same height all along, have given it an even row of battlements, and have broken the surface of the wall by two oriel windows. Formerly

[1] " The lower chamber, joyning to the bay-tree, in the first quadrangle," is said by Antony Wood to have always belonged to the Warden till Sir Thomas Clayton's time ; "the bay-tree" was the name of the first-floor room on the staircase next the porter's lodge, and the allocation of the adjoining room to the Warden may have been a reminiscence of the time when he held it as his official residence.

the eastward half of the front was a much
lower building ; this was called the Refectory, and a picture of it is given in
Loggan's print of the College, and later by
Skelton.[1]   It was remodelled at the time
of the restoration of the north front, when
the entrance from the street to the Warden's
lodgings was constructed.   Its walls were
slightly raised and ornamented with battlements to correspond with the adjoining
buildings.   Its interesting roof, probably of
the early fifteenth century, still remains in
excellent preservation.

Proceeding further east we reach St.
Alban Hall.   The old buildings, erected in
1599, were recently found to be in a very
insecure condition, and it has been necessary
to take down the greater part of them.   Indeed nothing now remains but the interesting old gateway and the lower part of the
street front.   Still further east were the
Principal's lodgings, largely rebuilt by Archbishop Whately, when Principal of the
Hall.   They were of a poor character, un-
attractive without and inconvenient within,
and were demolished in 1904 to make way
for additional College rooms.

Turning west and entering the College
Gate we find ourselves in the Front Quadrangle.   This has altered more than any
part of the College, and the only side which
remains as it was when it was first built is
the west, which is taken up by the east end

[1] *Oxonia antiqua restaurata*, Oxford, 1823, vol. ii.

of the Chapel and the Sacristy. Every
visitor will of course notice the Chapel

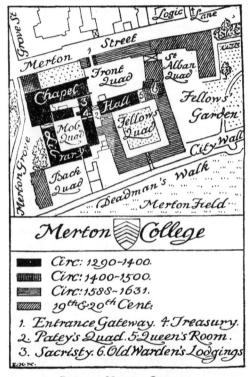

PLAN OF MERTON COLLEGE

window with its splendid broad arch and
magnificent tracery ; he should also notice

21

the quaint sun-dial at the north-east corner, the index of which is formed by the Chapel buttress.

The south side is occupied by the College Hall; as we see it now it looks a quite modern building; but although it has been re-faced, re-buttressed, re-roofed, and furnished with a new porch and steps (the porch was built in 1579, but altered later), the main walls may be as early as anything in the College, and were possibly built in the Founder's lifetime; at any rate in the Bursar's rolls of 1304 "the steps of the Hall" are mentioned, as if it had been some time in existence; and in 1330 the "louvre" over it was repaired. The big door should be noted; it is said to have been originally at the College porch; it dates from the fourteenth century, and the iron hinges and ornamentation belong to the best period of workmanship in England, and are hardly to be surpassed anywhere for beauty of design; the thinness of the oak planks which have lasted so many centuries is also a testimony to the care with which the wood was chosen.

The Hall itself has been as much restored within as without; little of the original work can be seen except the deep window seats, which were laid bare in the restoration of 1874 by Sir Gilbert Scott. The present fine timber roof then took the place of an ugly plaster ceiling; the windows, not very beautiful even now, took the place of others

still plainer; the musicians' gallery at the
west end, which had been for a long time
blocked up and used as an undergraduate's
set of rooms, was opened out; and the
present panelling was added, the coats of
arms (of eminent members and benefactors)
being presented by Warden Brodrick.
The walls were wainscotted with "linen-
pattern" oak panelling in 1540; but this
was removed during Wyatt's alterations at
the end of the eighteenth century.

At the east end of the Hall is a door
in the panel; that has been made quite
recently, but with it is connected an interesting incident in the history of the
College. When Charles I. and his court
arrived at Oxford in 1642 after the battle of
Edgehill, the King resided at Christ Church;
Queen Henrietta Maria, who joined him in
1643, was lodged in the Warden's house at
Merton, and occupied for nearly a year
the room over the archway, which is still
called "the Queen's room," with the adjoining room; both these rooms are now fitted
up as Common Rooms. That the King
and Queen might visit each other with
privacy a door was made from the "Queen's
room" into the Hall, from the other end of
which there was access through the passage
and archway over "Patey's Quad" into
the Sacristy, and thence into the Chapel;
from the south-west door of the Chapel
again a path was made through the grove,
south of the old buildings of Corpus, to

Christ Church, where the doorway can still be seen in the east wall of the garden belonging to the Professor of Pastoral Theology. The door from the Queen's room into the Hall was afterwards closed up, it is not certain when ; Chalmers, writing in 1810,[1] could say : " A passage has been described, that led from the Warden's lodgings to the Hall, and thence to the Vestry and Chapel, for her Majesty's accommodation in bad weather ; but it is not now visible." In the recent alterations of the Queen's room, however, the marks of the door were discovered, and it was opened out in 1904; it will now serve as the usual entrance into the Hall from the new Common Room.

Coming out of the Hall we face the north side of the Front Quadrangle ; there is little to be said about these buildings which has not already been said in describing the street front. It is, however, worth while to notice the difference in shape between the early attic window (1631) on the staircase west of the porter's lodge, and the restored windows behind the battlements in the rest of the building ; and further to the right the unevenness of height and projection shows where the old Refectory succeeds to the other College buildings ; the large windows are modern, but, if the engraving in Skelton is to be trusted, reproduce the lines of the old Refectory windows. It is on

[1] *History of Oxford*, p. 13.

the east side that the most modern part
of the College shows itself; this side has,
however, more than once been rebuilt.
According to the earliest engravings we
possess, such as Loggan's picture in 1675,
there ran a series of low buildings from
the east end of the Refectory to the
Warden's house, and a few feet in front
of them a fairly high wall; unfortunately,
artists who have since drawn the Quadrangle have naturally faced west so as to
give the view of the Chapel and Tower,
and the entries as to alterations in the
College Register are as a rule short and
meagre; and thus it is extremely hard to
discover what alterations were made in
these buildings till quite modern times.
There seem to have been, however, two
small buildings adjoining the Warden's
Tower, one of which was possibly Warden Sever's private chapel; and then another building connecting them with the
Refectory; this may possibly have been
the "College Gallery"[1] in which a sump-
tuous banquet was given by Warden Brent
to the French and Dutch ambassadors and

[1] Yet soon after this time, by the "long gallery" is
meant a gallery going south from the Warden's lodgings along the upper floor of the east side of the
Fellows' Quad. In Antony Wood's time it apparently extended along the whole east side; for he
complained of Warden Clayton building a summer-
house, "because it joyned almost to the long gallery,
the large bay-window whereof at its south-end affords
a farr better prospect than that of the summer-house"
(*Life and Times*, i. p. 396).

25

a number of the nobility when King Charles I. first visited Oxford in 1629. In 1836–38 these buildings were made uniform and turned into a gallery connecting the Warden's lodgings with Merton Street, into which the front door, now half blocked up, was made; and later, in 1882, the wall in front of them was removed. The final alterations of 1904–5 have given the Quadrangle the form which we trust it will preserve for centuries; the whole of the gallery and other buildings have been swept away, and a new side containing sets of rooms has been built in its place. This does something to relieve what has long been one of the most pressing needs of Merton, increased accommodation for undergraduates—a need which has also driven the College reluctantly to take the step, new in Oxford though not unknown in Cambridge, of building lodgings for the Warden on the opposite side of Merton Street.

The new buildings, which have been designed by Mr. Basil Champneys, are rather higher than the old, the level of the old gallery being preserved in the room over the archway leading into the St. Alban Hall Quadrangle; the style is Renaissance, and more in accord with the features of the Fellows' Quad than with those of the other parts of the College. At present they look painfully new to those whose eyes have been accustomed to the old

Warden's gallery, dark with age and smoke where the stone (or plaster) could be seen, but more than half covered with ivy and Virginia creeper, which in the autumn showed a glorious contrast of crimson and light green. But from the point of view of architecture there cannot be a moment's doubt that the new work is superior; and the gallery was after all not so very old, and was imitation Gothic poorly designed and badly built; it looked picturesque because so little of it was seen; and almost any building covered with creepers will look good in the spring and autumn. A few years of Oxford climate will tone down the white face of the newly erected buildings, and the Front Quadrangle will look as harmonious, and almost as old, as ever.

In the south-east corner stand the old Warden's lodgings. These were begun by Warden Henry Sever (1455-71), whose magnificent· sepulchral brass is one of the glories of the Chapel; but the work was completed by a later Warden, Richard Fitzjames (1483-1507), whose arms, a dolphin, may be seen in many parts of the College. The squat Tower, the archway with the "Queen's room" over it, and the two rooms with their bow windows looking out into the Fellows' Quad—in fact all that we can see from outside—date from his time. The recent alterations disclosed the fact that previous

builders had so ruthlessly cut away the
lower walls of the Tower, in order to
open up doorways or passages, that it
was a wonder it had not come down
long ago; there was also brought to light
a narrow winding staircase in the turret;
this is preserved, the walls have been
strengthened, and we trust that a new
lease of life is secured to the Tower.
Over the archway is a nice little piece
of carving representing two monks supporting a shield (Warden Fitzjames'), surmounted by a mitre; but the fine bold
gargoyles and corbels above are gradually
succumbing to age and the atmosphere.
The groined vaulting under the archway
into the Fellows' Quad has some quaint
carving; the twelve signs of the zodiac
appear at the intersection of the ribs, with
the royal arms and supporters of Henry VII.
in the centre; Libra is represented by a
judge in his robes.

Moving east under the new archway,
we find ourselves in the handsome three-
sided Quadrangle now approaching com-
pletion, with its pleasant view south into
the Fellows' Garden. We suppose that
this will still retain its old title of "St.
Alban Hall Quad," usually abbreviated to
"Stubbins" by the junior members of the
College.

To gain an idea of what St. Alban Hall
used to be we have quite a number of prints,
from Loggan downwards, giving us the

Merton Street front; the main changes
that have taken place there from Loggan's
time to 1904 have been in the attic
windows and in the Principal's house.
To get an idea of what the Quad was
like on the inside we must go to Mr.
Henderson's book, where, facing p. 138,
we see the north and the west sides.
It was a tiny little Quad, the south and
east sides of which were occupied by
modern and rather mean-looking buildings;[1]
but the view given in Mr. Henderson's
book is charmingly picturesque and old-
world. To the extreme left is seen a part
of the old Warden's House; in front the
one ancient piece of building in the Hall,
the Tower, surmounted by the quaint
projecting storey, called "the Dove-cot."
The Tower contained sets of rooms, and
the north side the Dining Hall, with sets
of rooms above it. This rubble Tower
was popularly supposed to date from the
beginning of the Hall's history, in which
case it would be as old as anything in
Merton; but all is uncertain, as we possess
very few documents relating to St. Alban
Hall's buildings. Small as the Hall was, it
must originally have been even smaller, as
apparently there were two Halls occupying
the site, St. Alban Hall and Nun Hall
(see below, p. 75).

Leaving the Front Quad by the south-

[1] The south side was rebuilt in 1789 by the Principal,
Dr. F. Randolph : see Ackerman, ii. p. 204.

west corner, we pass under an arch formed
by the passage connecting the Hall with
the Sacristy, built about the beginning of
the sixteenth century,[1] and come into a
small flagged court known to members of
the College as "Patey's Quad" from the
name of an old College servant who long
reigned there; then moving to the right
we are under another archway with the
door into the Treasury and Sacristy on our
right, and on the left the set of rooms once
occupied by the great Oxford antiquary,
Antony Wood; and then we enter the
oldest Quad in Oxford, "Mob Quad," or
as it always used to be called, "the Bachelors' Quad," or "the Little Quad." Here
we find ourselves in a College Quadrangle
very much as it must have been in the
fourteenth century; the dormer windows
on the south and west sides certainly date
from the beginning of the seventeenth, and
the windows on the ground and first floors
may have been enlarged after the original
date; the arched door into the Library must
belong to the fifteenth or sixteenth century;
the attic windows were renovated within
living memory; the strong doors which
barred the Quad not only from the outside
world but from other parts of Merton have
disappeared, though the iron staples and
deep slots for the bolts are still visible; but
with these exceptions the Quad is much as

[1] By Warden Rawlyns (1508–22) according to
Antony Wood.

it was when first completed.[1] Fortunately; for the worst disaster that could have befallen it very nearly happened in 1861, when the Warden and Fellows seriously considered and nearly adopted a proposal for enlarging the accommodation in College which would have involved the entire demolition of Mob Quadrangle to make room for a fine new Quad by Mr. Butterfield! No doubt the College was hemmed in by the City wall on the south, by Merton Street on the north, by Corpus on the west, and by St. Alban Hall on the east; but still it is not without a shudder that we think of the architect who urged this piece of vandalism and of those College Fellows who voted for it, and who all "died peacefully in their beds" as an Irish orator once indignantly remarked when describing some equally nefarious transaction.

The most interesting part of Mob Quad is the room over the arch by which we have entered it; this is the old Treasury, also called the "Exchequer." Tradition makes it older than the College, and asserts it to have been the identical house belonging to Jacob the Jew, which Walter of Merton bought (see p. 7); but though it may occupy the site of that house it is undoubtedly of the same date as the north and east sides of the Quad, that is of the early

[1] The theory that the north side was not added till the sixteenth century must certainly be rejected : see Henderson, p. 255 *f.*

31

fourteenth century. Noticeable from outside are the extremely strong walls, and the
high-pitched stone roof, supported on the

NORTH-EAST CORNER OF MOB QUAD, SHOWING
THE STONE ROOF OF THE TREASURY

inside not by wooden beams, but by arches
few in number and at uneven intervals, so
that it is not easy to see how it has kept
together; yet there it is, one of the oldest

32

strong rooms in England, as sound now as the day on which it was finished.

A winding staircase from the outer Sacristy leads into the room. In it are stored the various Merton archives, many of them of the greatest value not only for the history of the College but for the history of England.[1] There are the title-deeds of the College property,[2] and the Bursars' Rolls with their details of current income and expenditure ; the various Catalogues of Fellows, the earliest dating from the reign of Henry V.; and the official College Register, beginning with the year 1482 and continuing up to the present day, and giving a valuable account of College Meetings and of other incidents in its domestic history ; the latter has been carefully indexed.[3]

But though the Treasury is not earlier than the College, it is probably, with the two sides enclosing it, the earliest part of Mob Quad. A little observation will make it clear that the stone of the north and east sides is somewhat different from that

[1] It was to the Merton Bursars' Rolls that the late Professor Thorold Rogers was largely indebted for the information digested in his *History of Prices in England.*

[2] Only a few years ago, in 1903, the College was able, through the kindness of Bodley's Librarian, to add to its collection a deed of a grant of land in Durham dated 1284.

[3] A good description of many of these documents is given in the Introduction to Brodrick's *Memorials of Merton.*

of the other sides, and it may well be that a generation or more separates the two. Old though the Quad is, it does not look so ancient as many Oxford buildings which are centuries later; and this is largely due to the fact that it was built of stone from Teynton, before the discovery of the quarries at Headington; it is the Headington stone which so soon turns black and crumbles away, gives a fine old-world look to the buildings, but nearly breaks the hearts of College Bursars.

The wise visitor will not leave Mob Quad without going to the south-east corner, from which he will gain a fine view of the College Tower, which, however, looks its best just at the time when few visitors can see it, *i.e.* on a moonlight night in the vacation, when the lower buildings are shrouded in darkness and the white light gleams on pinnacle, battlement, and window with almost unearthly grandeur. If he is wise too, the visitor will refrain from walking through the south passage into the "Back Quad" which contains the buildings erected by Mr. Butterfield in 1864, and for which the trees of the beautiful Merton Grove were sacrificed; they are so ugly that at any rate we may be thankful we have no more of them. From the Back Quad, however, a good view of the Chapel transept and tower may be obtained over the roof line of Mob Quad; and there may also be seen the pleasant set of ground floor rooms next the archway, which were occupied by Lord Randolph Churchill when he was an undergraduate member of the College.

But if Mr. Butterfield's buildings are the

THE LIBRARY FROM THE BACK QUAD

ugliest in Oxford, we may pride ourselves in having the most beautiful thing in Oxford or even England in our Library. There is perhaps no interior which seems to transport us so immediately into a

bygone age as the Merton Library. It was
built in the latter part of the fourteenth
century (1377–78) by William Rede,
Bishop of Chichester, who had formerly
been a Fellow of the College; but it is
not certain whether he built, or rebuilt, the
entire two sides of the Quadrangle over
which the Library now extends, or whether
he simply added to already existing buildings.

Entering by the main door, we mount the
staircase and find ourselves at the angle
formed by the south and west wings, this
junction being technically termed the "vestibule." Turning to the right, we find
ourselves in the oldest part of the Library;
the greater part of the fittings, book-cases
and reading-counters, benches and foot-rests,
tiling in the centre and wooden floor at the
sides, and glass in the east windows, are probably of the fourteenth century. No wonder
the rows of double book-cases, forming as
they do a series of recesses, each lighted by
a narrow lancet window, have given rise to
the tradition that the room was originally
a dormitory; it seems to be divided into a
number of cubicles; but the researches of
Mr. Henderson [1] and of Mr. J. W. Clark [2]
have shown that the dormitory system was
unknown in the Colleges at Oxford and
Cambridge, and that a simpler explanation
is the right one. Many of the early monastic libraries were built on this pattern,

[1] See *History of Merton College*, p. 229 f.
[2] See *The Care of Books*, chaps. iv. and v.

and consisted of a long room lighted by a number of narrow windows between which were placed at right angles not book-cases but desks, something like elongated double lecterns ; on the sloping sides of these were placed the manuscripts chained to a rod either at the top or the bottom, but ready for use without being moved from their place.[1] It is obvious that such a system, however, would accommodate very few volumes, at most three or four to a desk ; and as books increased, a simple method of economising space was obtained, by making the desks horizontal, multiplying their number by three or four, and storing the books on end.

The books would be chained as before, but placed in the shelves the reverse way to a modern library ; not a few of the older books at Merton have their press-marks on the front edge of the leaves instead of the back. Then the reading-counters would be added and the books when in use placed on them. The result of this alteration of the lectern into the book-case has been most happy ; the Merton Library very probably gave the pattern to Oxford of a system of storing books which both economised space and looked pictur-esque, while the recesses formed a series of delightful semi-private studies.

Examining the west wing more closely,

[1] Many of the Merton MSS. have their titles written on the side of their covers, showing that they were originally kept on desks and not in shelves.

A Recess in the Library

38

we note that though the book-cases show every mark of great age, the little Jacobean ornaments on the tops belong to the beginning of the seventeenth century ; the beautiful dormer windows are of the same date, as are also the delightfully quaint ornamental arches which divide the vestibule both from the west and from the south wings. The panelling at the end of the west wing and the elaborate plaster work above, date from the middle of the seventeenth century ; the English joiners had at this time found out the art of making "mitred" joints, and were so pleased with the discovery that they inserted as many right angles as possible in order to show off their "mitres" ; the extreme beauty of the door in this panelling should be noticed. In the plaster work above are three coats of arms ; in the middle that of the College,[1] on the left that of Archbishop Whitgift (Abp. of Canterbury,

---

[1] The College arms are, on a shield or, three chevrons, per pale counterchanged azure and gules. These are the Founder's arms and are slightly modified from those of Clare, Walter of Merton obtaining permission to bestow the Manors of Malden and Farleigh on his College from the feudal lord Richard de Clare, Earl of Gloucester.

The above shield is, however, often represented as parted per pale with that of the see of Rochester (argent, on a saltire gules, an escallop or), when the Merton arms occupy the sinister and the Rochester arms the dexter sides of the shield. This is the shield of the Founder *as Bishop of Rochester;* and as the College has no real connection with Rochester, it is very doubtful whether it should use these arms: see Henderson, p. 293.

1583–1604), and on the right that of Sir Henry Savile (Warden 1586–1622). The ceiling (a " waggon " roof) dates from the beginning of the sixteenth century, and the Tudor rose and Warden Fitzjames' dolphin can be seen in its ornamentation. I the ends of the book-cases are examined carefully they will be seen to have pieces of wood of a later date inserted into them ; these take the places of the locks and bars by which the books used to be chained. Rods ran the length of each case and were kept in their sockets on the outer end by flat iron bars hinged above and locked below ; the books were secured by chains to the rods, and in order to remove a book the bar at the end would have to be unlocked and raised, and the rod pulled out. Narrow slits were cut in the reading-counters for the slack part of the chain to fall down while the books were in use. The chains were not removed from the Library till 1792, and it is a thousand pities that the outside bars and locks were removed at the same time ; only a half-case, the first on the left hand in the south wing, has been left with one rod, lock and chains to show what the whole Library must once have been.

The south wing of the Library looks more modern. The book-cases are of the same pattern as the other wing, but are slightly larger, the oak not so dark and the edges sharper. In 1623 the whole of this wing was remodelled ; a separate room at the east end was thrown into the Library, the two dormer windows on the north side and the large oriel window in the east wall were constructed, the old book-cases sold, and a joiner named Benet commissioned to supply twenty new cases and one half-case. It will be observed, however, that though the cases are comparatively modern, the reading-counters and benches are of much older wood and are not even planed, but simply smoothed with an adze ; it looks, therefore, as if the joiner had saved trouble and expense by using up the still serviceable pieces of the old furniture. In the oriel window are twelve beautifully quaint cartoons of Dutch glass bearing the date 1598 ; they contain a strange mixture of the sacred and the profane, as the main subjects are scenes from our Lord's Passion, while each picture is flanked by figures representing the virtues and vices, the senses, and characters from classical history and mythology ; the representation of the Crucifixion is actually flanked by Venus on one side and Lucretia on the other. Old though the pictures are, they are a recent acquisition to the Library, and the glass around them is quite modern ; they were presented to the Library in 1841 by the Rev. E. T. Bigge, Fellow and Librarian, and afterwards Archdeacon of Lindisfarne. The donor immortalised himself in another way, by compiling a recipe for a brew of strong ale, famous still in Merton (though no longer brewed in the

Sacristy), and known as "Archdeacon." Underneath the window is a case of astrological instruments; of these one astrolabe is dated 1560, but the other is mediæval, and may possibly have been used by Chaucer. The proclamation of King Charles I. about the ship-money has been recently framed and put into a prominent position in the Library, but has probably been in the College since it was sent there in 1640.

Under the south window of the vestibule is another glass case containing some of the illuminated manuscripts in which the College is fairly rich. The two globes, with their handsome mahogany stands, date from the late sixteenth century, a time when globes were considered a necessary part of the furniture of every College Library.

The ghost of Duns Scotus is said to haunt the Library; but the present writer, though he has been in it at various times of the day and night, cannot claim to have seen him, and the historical difficulties are serious if not insuperable. For, as we shall see, it is extremely improbable that Duns Scotus was ever a member of the College; even if he was, he died at Cologne; and he died in 1308, seventy years before the Library was built.

If the Library is picturesque, the Chapel is grand; the amount of enthusiasm felt for it is a good sign of the architectural taste and education of a visitor. The Choir, built at the finest period of Gothic architecture (probably 1290-1300 [1]), when the Early English school was developing into the Decorated, stands almost unrivalled in its combination of simplicity and grace. The Early English builders aimed at severe beauty of proportion and general design, and in their windows confined themselves to the lancet and circular, trefoil, or quatrefoil light, arranging these in many varieties of combination ; but their immediate successors, the architects of the Early Decorated school, began to allow themselves one piece of indulgence—window tracery. In this they revelled, and the Merton windows are a specimen of the earlier and more sober period of their revels. Here the tracery is beautiful and yet severe ; severer at the sides of the Choir than at the east end where the breadth of the great window and the complexity of its geometrical patterns are really astonishing.

Window tracery naturally enough began with the geometrical pattern ; that is a simple development of the double lancet with a circle or quatrefoil above it ; and so the Merton tracery is mainly geometrical. Four patterns sufficed for the fourteen side windows, but each is almost perfect in its proportions, and each is entirely distinct from the others. The patterns are the same on each side of the Choir ; starting from the west end, the first four windows north and

[1] This is the probable date, though it may have been begun as early as 1277 : see Henderson, p. 196.

43

south have four separate patterns, and the fifth, sixth, and seventh reproduce respectively the first, second, and third. But while the builders were compelled to keep the side windows narrow by the number of buttresses necessary for supporting the walls and roof, at the east end they had the whole breadth of the Chapel at their disposal ; there was no roof pressure here pushing the wall out in the middle ; a buttress at each corner was sufficient for keeping the side walls in their place, and the rest of the space was not needed structurally ; it could be arched over with a big span and filled in with glass and elaborate devices in stone.

If the east window of the Chapel shows us geometrical tracery at its best, the two east windows of the Sacristy next door are probably the earliest known examples of another development from Early English, that into curvilinear tracery. The lower lights of these windows terminate in what are called *ogee* arches, and the curves of these arches being continued till they reached the window arch, a beautiful net-like effect was produced, which has earned for this kind of tracery the technical name of "reticulated." In time the reticulated work developed into the flamboyant, of which such superb specimens are to be seen in France ; but in the Merton sacristy we see the beginning of it all.

One more feature of the outside of the Choir should be noticed—the gargoyles on

the north side, meant to carry off the water
from the roof; most of them unfortunately have suffered from the weather, and
are crumbling away; but enough can be
seen to imagine what huge grotesque figures
they must have appeared long ago as on
some showery day they vomited the water
from their mouths and held their hands to
their heads or chests as if they were in the
throes of sea-sickness.

On entering we find ourselves in the
transepts, which are the latest part of the
Chapel, though some parts of the south
transept may date back as early as the
thirteenth or beginning of the fourteenth
century ; [1] the rest was added later, the
whole being finished about 1425, and the
Tower completed in 1451. The transepts
are splendidly lofty, and the Tower arches
very grand ; but if they are examined carefully it will be seen that the work is
uneven, that the north and south windows
do not correspond either in size or tracery,
and that the broad west window does not
really fit the arch into which it has been
inserted, while the west wall contains
arches both north and south which have
been filled up with stone. All this points
to gradual building and extensive alteration
of plans. The design of adding a nave
to the Chapel was at one time entertained,
but was afterwards dropped ; why, is not

[1] The piscina in the south transept is Early Decorated
work : see Henderson, p. 202 f.

clear. Popular tradition indeed ascribes
the form of most College Chapels—a choir
with two transepts but no nave—to the

SOUTH TRANSEPT OF THE CHAPEL FROM
THE GROVE

happy accident of Merton having found
itself unable to complete its Chapel. But
the Chapel of New College, which is defi-

46

nitely designed on this plan, was finished
in 1386, several years before the west
windows were put into the Merton ante-
chapel ; and so William of Wykeham must
enjoy the honour of designing the ideal
form for a College Chapel, and Merton must
have followed his example, either from admiration or from financial reasons. Still
the roof line and arches bear witness even
now to the magnificent church which Merton once contemplated erecting ; contem-
plations on the subject, however, were put
a stop to by the foundation of Corpus Christi
College in 1515, and it is somewhat humili-
ating to reflect that the greater part of the
land on which the next-door neighbour
stands was Merton property, and was sold
to Bishop Foxe by the Warden (Richard
Rawlyns) for an annuity of £4, 6s. 8d. ;
for this, however, Warden Rawlyns was de-
prived by the Visitor, Archbishop Warham.

Turning east from the transept, we enter
the Choir through some poor brass gates in
an equally poor dwarf stone wall ; these
are modern, and were erected in 1851.
And, to pass over the less interesting
features of the Chapel at once, we may say
that the Choir stalls, tapestry on the walls,
tiles on the floor, altar rails, and roof, are
the product of restorations undertaken
between 1842 and 1876.

Fortunately a good deal remains belonging to the earliest days of the College.
If the tracery of the Choir windows com-

mands our admiration from the outside, the glass commands it when we are inside. It is rare that painted glass of so early a date has been preserved so completely; save that the lower parts of the windows near the sanctuary have been pieced here and there with new glass, and that two or three of the kneeling figures have been filled up with Messrs. Powell's work, the side windows are just as they were when first fitted with glass by Henry of Mamesfield, Fellow of Merton from 1288 to 1328. The middle light of each window contains one of the apostles, and the side lights show a kneeling figure with a scroll bearing the legend, "Magister Henricus de Mamesfeld me fecit;"[1] in the decoration on some of the windows may also be seen the portrait of Elinor of Castile, the first wife of Edward I., and the Castile arms, consisting of three castles. As Queen Elinor died in 1290, this approximately fixes the date of the windows. Yet such very early painted glass is almost more interesting than beautiful; glass-painting matured later than architecture, and was in its zenith when architecture was declining; the big west window in the ante-chapel is a piece of quite ordinary perpendicular work; but the fragments of glass preserved in it are superb

[1] The new panels may be distinguished, if the visitor is unable otherwise to detect the difference between old glass and a very fair modern imitation, by the scroll having the inscription, "Fratres Powell me fecerunt."

48

in their depth and richness of colour ;[1] and had the side windows received their glass in the fifteenth instead of the thirteenth century, they would be less important historically, but far more effective. Unfortunately the east window remains as a terrible witness to the fact that glass-painting ultimately declined, and declined very much ; the lower lights with their six scenes from the life of our Lord were the work of a certain W. Price, and were inserted in 1702 at the expense of a former Fellow, Mr. A. Fisher, during the Wardenship of Richard Lydall. The Chapel windows, therefore, give us specimens of the rise, the reign, and the fall of English glass-painting.

The two corbels of the east window are hardly distinguishable save on a bright morning ; but they are portraits respectively of the Founder (north) and of Edward I. (south). The visitor will have noticed from outside, though it is even more noticeable inside, that the window begins at a very low level ; even the frame of the picture over the altar hides some of it. This is a thoroughly English characteristic, and may be constantly seen in the east windows of our parish churches. Conservative in many things, the mediæval English builders clung to the old idea that the principal object in the Church should be the altar, not the altar-

[1] Notice especially the beautiful figure of an Abbess holding a pastoral staff; traditionally said to be St. Scholastica.

piece. Lofty and elaborate reredoses, such
as are seen so often abroad, were rare ; and
though Oxford contains at New College
and All Souls splendid specimens of these,
yet they were there due to a very simple
reason. William of Wykeham conceived
the plan, afterwards adopted in other Colleges, of occupying one side of his Quadrangle with the Chapel and Hall, in such
a way that the east wall of the Chapel
formed the west wall of the Hall ; this of
course rendered the insertion of an east
window in the Chapel impossible, and it
became necessary to cover the bare surface
of wall with a wealth of niches and statuary.
But these were exceptional, and, beautiful as
they are, they tend to distract the attention
of the worshipper ; the altar becomes a small
feature in the reredos, instead of the reredos
a small screen at the back of the altar ; the
low level of the majority of east windows
shows that as a rule only some three or four
feet were allowed for decoration above the
holy table. The picture forming our altar-
piece was given in 1779 by John Skipp, a
gentleman-commoner of the College ; it is a
finely grouped picture of the Crucifixion,
and if not actually by Tintoretto, is at least
a good imitation of his style. The massive
silver candlesticks were presented in 1706
by the Hon. E. Watson. The roof was a
timber " waggon " roof, as may be seen in
the older pictures of the Chapel ; the present
roof was adorned and painted in 1850 under

the personal supervision of one of the Fellows, Mr. J. H. Pollen, and it harmonises well with the rest of the building. The magnificent brass lectern [1] was a legacy from John Martok, a Fellow, who died in 1458, though for some unknown reason the lectern was not placed in the College Chapel till 1504 ; it bears the inscription, " Orate pro anima magistri iohannis martok," and has Warden Fitzjames' dolphin on each side. The expression on the faces of the lions at the pedestal should be observed.

Of other decoration both Chapel and ante-chapel are singularly bare ; they gain their effect from height and proportion, from the grandeur of their arches and the beauty of their windows. But of monumental brasses there is still a good number, though, as the empty matrices in the ante-chapel show, not nearly so many as once were there. On Oct. 17, 1655, the roof of the south transept suddenly fell in and broke a good many of the monumental stones on the floor ; Antony Wood, however, " retriev'd the brass plates that were fixed on them, and transcrib'd and sav'd the inscriptions on them;" but during repairs in Chapel a few years later (1659) the workmen tore up and stole several of the brasses, and though Wood " complayn'd of these things to the fellowes, . . . with shame be it spoken, not one of them did resent the

<hr>

[1] Ingram in his *Memorials of Oxford*, vol. i. p. 25*n.*, boldly describes it as " a large brasen eagle ! "

matter, or enquire after the sacrilegists, such were their degenerated and poore spirits"; however, he had preserved and published the inscriptions.[1]

Of the brasses now surviving, the two finest are in the Choir just below the Sanctuary steps, that on the north side to John Bloxham (Warden 1375–87) and John Whytton (Rector of Wootton and benefactor to the College), that on the south to Warden Sever (†1471). The first has two small full-length figures on a canopied bracket, and is very graceful in design; the second is a full-length figure almost life size, under a canopy and richly ornamented, the embroidery on the cope being especially noticeable. These brasses were removed from the ante-chapel, where the original matrices may be seen, and laid in the Choir in 1849. They had far better have been left alone; so clumsily were they cemented and screwed into their new slabs that they began to crack and were rapidly getting into a ruinous condition; in 1905 they were carefully relaid again by Messrs. Barkentin and Krall, and are now sound and smooth as of old.

In the ante-chapel the two half-lengths in the south transept commemorate John Kyllyngworth (†1445) and John Bowk (†1519); the latter is pictured holding a chalice with the host inside; these were

[1] Wood, *Life and Times*, i. pp. 199, 309; they were printed in his *History*.

removed a few years ago from their old position in front of the Choir gates, where they were getting badly worn. In the north transept should be noted the fine mutilated brass of Richard de Hakeborne (†c. 1311), consisting of a half-effigy in the head of a Greek cross with a marginal inscription in Lombardic characters; Hakeborne was one of the first Fellows of the College, and this brass is said to be the sixth oldest in England. Near to it is another brass supposed to be that of either Warden Trenge (†1351) or Warden Durant (†1375); all that remains now is a small figure in the head of a floriated cross.

Of mural monuments, those of Sir Henry Savile (Warden 1586–1622) and Sir Thomas Bodley (†1613) are respectively on the south and north of the west wall; they were originally eastward in the Choir, but were removed in the last restoration; their florid classical ornamentation does not after all harmonise so badly with the Gothic work around them, and Savile's monument is interesting as containing below the bust pictures of Eton College and of Merton, as they were in the early part of the seventeenth century. On the east wall of the north transept, just by the door, is the monument of Antony Wood (†1695); and in the slabs to Bishop Patteson (†1871) and in the south transept to F. St. Clair Grimwood (†1891) the College commemorates two of her members who died as heroes should, the one as a Christian martyr in Melanesia, the other as a loyal servant of his country in the rising at Manipur.

Two pieces of Church furniture attract attention as being strange in a College Chapel; the pulpit and the font. They point back to the time when the Chapel was also a Parish Church, as has been mentioned above (p. 7). The Parish services took place in the ante-chapel, and permission to use the Choir and Altar for Communion was granted as an act of grace by the College; and during some years following the Oxford Movement, when feeling on ritual questions ran high, the Vicar of St. John the Baptist's was threatened by his less advanced brother Fellows with exclusion from the Choir. Thus the Merton Chapel began as a Parish Church, continued as a College Chapel and Parish Church combined, and is now a College Chapel only.

The north transept window and outside front were repaired during 1902, as they had got in a dangerous condition; but the two statues, of St. John the Baptist and the Virgin Mary, were carefully protected, and as much of the old carving preserved as possible; these statues, according to Antony Wood, were set up by Warden Fitzjames (*City of Oxford*, i. p. 175).

The Chapel looks fine at all times;

54

on a summer evening the sun streaming
through the big west window lights it
with a splendid glow of colour and re-
veals ever new beauties in the painted
glass; but perhaps the effect in the winter
is even finer. On a Sunday evening the
twinkling candles light the stalls and shine
on the surplices of the Fellows and Postmasters; the glass of the east window is
fortunately invisible, but the stone tracery
comes out into prominence; all the upper
part of the Chapel is shrouded in most
magnificent gloom and the roof is almost
lost in the darkness.

The Tower has to yield to Magdalen
in height, nor has it the same opportunity
of showing its proportions clear of the
Chapel; it does not rise sheer from the
street, but only crowns the transept roof.
But though not so lofty or graceful as
Magdalen, it is broader and more massive;
viewed from the Cherwell or the Broad
Walk nothing can be finer than the dignified repose with which it rests among
the College buildings; and it harmonises
as well with the Fellows' Quadrangle as
with the Chapel; the combination of City
wall, College buildings, and garden foliage
would be perfect save for the discord, both
in form and colour, of the staring Butterfield block. Soon after 1422 there is
mention of the building of a Campanile,
but the present Tower was apparently
started in 1448 and finished about 1451.

If the accounts preserved in the Bursars'
Rolls give the complete expenditure, we
can only say that it is the cheapest piece
of building known to history, for the total
expenses both for materials and wages
are stated to have been just under £186;
even allowing for the greater value of
money in those days, this is wonderful;
and it is probable that much work must
have been done afterwards for which we
have no accounts preserved.

The Merton bells do not yield even
to Magdalen in resonance or sweetness;
they are one of the merriest peals that
can be heard, either when their sound is
mellowed by distance, or when the visitor
is close under them and they seem to
make the College Quad rock with their
splendid crashing. The tenor bell is one
of the finest in Oxford and weighs 27
cwt., the Cathedral tenor being very little
heavier; but the rest of the peal is worthy
of it, and forms, what is very rare with
such an old peal, an octave in almost perfect tune. Yet originally the bells, though
fewer, must have been much heavier; a
peal of five had belonged to the Chapel
since the early part of the fifteenth century, when Warden Henry Abyndon presented the tenor; some of the other bells
were very possibly inherited from the old
church. The tenor was a giant, and said
to weigh 50 cwt.; Antony Wood tells
us that it was supposed to be the best bell

in England, "being, as 'twas said, of fine
mettal silver found" (*i.e.* with a small
quantity of silver put in, when cast, to
improve the tone). In 1657 the five bells
had got into an unsatisfactory state, and
were recast into a peal of eight, but so
badly done that in 1680 they had to be
re-cast again by a famous bell-founder,
Christopher Hodson. Hodson had a foundry in London and a branch foundry at
St. Mary Cray, in Kent; the Merton
bells were probably cast in the London
foundry, and brought there and back by
water; and they were so well cast that
little has had to be done since.[1] The present ringers' gallery (not an easy one to ring
from) was made at the same time (1680),
though slight alterations have taken place
later.

Between Mob Quad and the Choir of the
Chapel is the Sacristy; there used to be
two doors into it, one from the Chapel and
one from Mob Quad, but the Chapel door
has been blocked up. Privileged persons
enter through the door under the Treasury,
and find themselves in a small stone vestibule, the outer Sacristy; on the left is the
staircase up to the Treasury, and in front
the door into the inner Sacristy. The
Sacristy is a little later than the Chapel,
as is shown by the obviously external buttress which projects into it; but College
entries exist showing that the foundations

[1] See Wood's *Life and Times*, i. p. 211, 219, ii. p. 515.

were begun in 1311, so it was building in that and possibly the next year.[1]

In the Sacristy were no doubt kept the vestments of the Chaplains and of those of the Fellows who were priests; possibly the superb cope belonging to Warden Sever was preserved in its semicircular chest; and there would also be the furniture of the altar and the vessels for Holy Communion. The little squint looking into the Chapel commands the High Altar, and through it the assistants could observe the Priest as he celebrated the Mass. Yet not so long ago this beautiful room was put to very base uses. In 1826 it was seriously proposed to turn it into the College bakehouse. In the following year the door connecting it with the Chapel was blocked up and it was actually converted into the College brewhouse, for which purpose it was used till 1878. Now, however, it is employed for a more dignified purpose. It was repaired, and a new timber roof and dormer windows added in 1886, and the College Collection of Manuscripts, some of which are of great beauty and value, was placed in cases round the walls. Still more recently some bookcases, modelled on those in the Library, have been placed there to accommodate the overflow of books. With the manuscripts is guarded one of Merton's great treasures, a copy of the first Caxton Chaucer.

The Fellows' Quadrangle does not need

[1] Henderson, pp. 200, 259.

a long description; it is, for Merton, comparatively modern, having been built at the beginning of the seventeenth century (1608–10); it is not easy to imagine what the College must have looked like from the south before it was built. It is a handsome Quad, and the gateway into the meadow resembles the famous "five-order" gate in the Bodleian buildings; but Merton has only four orders, Doric, Ionic, Corinthian, and Composite.

Large as the Quad is, it afforded till lately but few sets of rooms, though some of them are among the finest in Oxford.[1] But the north side is taken up by the Hall; kitchen common rooms and a lecture room absorb the greater part of the west, and the Warden's house and another lecture room occupied much of the east. The recent changes have added some nine sets of undergraduates' rooms on the east side, out of the old Warden's house; and another change that has come over the University in the last generation—the decay of the bachelor Don—has thrown open sets of rooms once sacred to Fellows for the occupation of undergraduates. The inhabitants of the Fellows' Quad are younger and more numerous than they used to be, and there may come a time when the very reason of its

[1] In Antony Wood's time the lodgings allotted to the Senior Fellow formed a set of six rooms, three upper rooms and three lower; but the lower rooms were annexed to the Warden's house by Sir Thomas Clayton (*Life and Times*, i. p. 396).

name will have been forgotten. The turf in this Quad was not added till 1838.

The old Senior Common Room, as we suppose it must be now called, has indeed a right to that title; for it is the oldest in Oxford. What seems to visitors one of the most characteristic features of University life, the adjournment of the Fellows to dessert in Common Room after dinner in Hall, is not really so very ancient. Certainly as late as the seventeenth century it was their custom to repair to various taverns in the City after dinner; and the position of the Common Rooms in the different Colleges, some near, others at a distance from their Halls, proves that they were no part of the original plan of the buildings; they were added later when room could be found or converted for their use.[1] Merton led the way in turning a large room over the kitchen into a Common Room in 1661; the oak wainscotting was added some ten years later. Seen in the daytime it is a rather gloomy room; but when lighted up on a winter evening, with the College silver shining on the dark mahogany table, few Common Rooms are more genial and cosy.

The Fellows' Garden is private, though undergraduates of the College may introduce friends into it during certain hours in the afternoon. Every College which possesses a garden boasts that it has the

[1] See Willis and Clark, *Archit. Hist. of Univ. of Cambridge*, iii. p. 381.

finest in Oxford; but though the Merton garden is small and without the wide expanses of lawn that distinguish Trinity or St. John's, its situation and the beauty of its trees give it a rare charm. The view of the Fellows' Quad from the end of the lime-avenue on a May morning; the south wall of that Quad when the roses are in bloom; the terrace in the calm of a summer evening when the moon is rising; when these have been seen once, or still better seen many times, they are not easily forgotten, and their remembrance will gild the most prosaic surroundings with a glamour of romance. Yet, as often at Oxford, the effect has not been designedly produced, but is the result of chance additions and changes during many centuries. The Warden's garden was originally the garden of St. Alban Hall; and the Fellows' garden with its lime-avenue, winding paths, and chestnut-shaded lawns, was divided up into narrow strips occupied by no less than six private halls. These were acquired by the College during the fifteenth century and the sites added to the College garden; but for two small strips of the ground, one just east of St. Alban Hall, and the other on the present east terrace, the College had to pay rent to Balliol and the City respectively till quite recent times.[1]

[1] The Balliol strip was bought in 1804 for £72; the City strip exchanged for a house in St. Aldate's in 1854.

The City wall which surrounds the south and east sides of the garden was, according to Antony Wood, once as high as it is at New College ; the Terrace, one of the most beautiful features of the garden, was not made till 1706–7 ; the trees along the north side were not planted till 1744. The slightly raised walk which runs from near the Terrace steps across to the St. Alban's Quad marks the division between the Fellows' garden and that which used to belong to the Warden. This was an inner garden, enclosed by walls south and east, so that the Fellows would have to walk along a passage from the Quad gate before they reached their own garden. These walls gave place to light iron railings in 1855 and 1859, and the railings themselves disappeared in 1904 when the Warden's garden was united to the Fellows'. The sun-dial was presented by Mr. George Tierney, Fellow, in 1830.

Loggan's engraving of Merton represents the Warden's garden as laid out in formal Italian style, with a tall summer-house at the south-east corner ; this was built during the Wardenship of Sir Thomas Clayton (1661–93), and at the desire of his wife, as Antony Wood, who hated Lady Clayton, takes care to inform us :—

"The warden's garden must be alter'd, new trees planted, arbours made, rootes of choice flowers bought, &c. All which tho unnecessary, yet the poore Coll. must pay for them, and all this to please a woman. Not content with these matters, there must be a new summer-house built at the south-end of the warden's garden, wherein her ladyship and her gossips may take their pleasure, and any eves-dropper of the family may harken what any of the fellows should accidentally talk of in the passage to their owne garden " (*Life and Times*, i. p. 396).

The Oxford Almanack for 1798 shows a summer-house in the same place but apparently of a different style. The present dilapidated summer-house on the east terrace was put up in 1706–7, and either here or in the path just outside the City wall (which is known as "Dead man's walk") Francis Windebank, a Colonel in the Royalist forces, was shot after a Court-Martial in 1645, for having surrendered Bletchingdon House to the Parliamentary troops at their first summons, and without a blow (see Carlyle's *Cromwell*, i. 213).

CHAPTER III

THE COLLEGE LIFE AND HISTORY

WE have described the constitution and the principal officers of the College as provided in Walter of Merton's Statutes; there is, however, one official mentioned in them whom we have only just named but who soon became a most important element in its life—the Visitor. The Visitor selected by the Founder in 1264 was the Bishop of Winchester, but since 1276 the Archbishop of Canterbury has held the office. With him lies the final appeal on such questions as the interpretation of the College Statutes, the expulsion of an unworthy member, or the settlement of a quarrel between those who have forgotten their Founder's exhortation to observe peace, concord, and love; he has the right of examining into the life of the College and of suggesting or insisting on reforms, such as the election of more Fellows and the proper allocation of College revenues; and it is indeed from the Injunctions of the Visitors that we gain much of our information as to the internal arrangements of the College and

Lectern *in the* Chapel

the daily life of its members during the Middle Ages.

Thus it is interesting to find in such Injunctions not only the regular monitions that the number of Fellows is to be kept up and their incomes kept down, and that they are to live at peace with the Warden and with each other, but also advice that they should never take meals in the town or enter it alone, but should always walk about in a body and return before night-fall.[1] In 1401 we have an order that every Fellow must take Holy Orders within three or four years after obtaining his degree in Arts. Archbishop Chicheley in 1425 issued very strict regulations as to the management of the College revenues ; the Fellowships were to be raised to forty-four in number, additional Chaplains appointed, wasteful sales of timber stopped, and the College accounts audited every year by some discreet person " being neither a Fellow nor a dependant of the College."

A similar insight into the College life is afforded by the record of one of the "Scrutinies," or Stated General Meetings as we should now call them, which by the Statutes were to be held three times a year ; at them inquiry was to be made into the conduct and diligence of the Fellows, complaints lodged, and offences punished. Some of the complaints at the Scrutiny of July

[1] Archb. Peckham's Injunctions, 1284 ; see Brodrick, *Memorials of Merton*, p. 26.

and December 1338, and March 1339, are amusing enough.[1] Robert Trenge was Warden, and it was alleged that one of the Fellows had publicly addressed him as " Robert " ; one Fellow had threatened to kill another ; there seems to have been constant quarrelling among them, and between them and the Warden ; and severe criticisms are passed upon the Chaplain's clothes and boots.

The College, therefore, was not always a united Society ; yet it would be unfair to take either the Visitors' Injunctions or the Scrutinies as giving a complete picture of its life, for these were just the occasions when complaints and little else were heard and rectified. But the number of Fellows who are stated to have made no complaints at the above Scrutiny is large ; and no doubt the majority got on well enough. It needed but a little opposition or encroachment from outside to unite them ; and they were not without this tonic for long. The right of Visitation belongs to the Archbishop himself, not to any deputy or substitute ; when the see of Canterbury is vacant, the Chapter can perform most of the Primate's functions but they cannot visit Merton College. In 1486 they tried and failed ; the College vigorously resisted their claim and obtained the advice of an eminent jurist, Dr. Jane, who, after giving various reasons against the jurisdiction

[1] *Memorials of Merton*, p. 341 f.

claimed by the Chapter, finished his letter with the following sound practical advice ; should the Prior of Canterbury appear before the College "let hyme doo withowt the gates of your college what hym lykith, and barre your gates fast, and let hyme not cume in butt in the similitude of a good fellow to essay your ale, not to vysite."

In 1562 there occurred an open rupture between the Senior Fellows, who were opposed to the Reformation, and Archbishop Parker. They had put themselves in the wrong by presenting five candidates for the office of Warden, instead of three, as the College Statutes ordained ; and Parker taking advantage of this claimed the right of appointment himself, and nominated one of his own chaplains, Mr. John Mann. The new Warden's entrance into the College was resisted by some of the Fellows, one of whom (Mr Hall), according to Antony Wood, boxed his ears "for his presumption to enter into the gates without his leave." But this time the College had to submit ; Parker issued a Commission to inquire into the matter, Mann was established in the Wardenship, Hall expelled from the College, and the anti-Reformation party amongst the Fellows broken up. In the next century the College fared no less hardly at the hands of Archbishop Laud ; his Visitation was long and thorough and his ordinances regulated the minutest details of daily life. Not only the Fellows, but Junior Masters,

Bachelors and Scholars were to attend chapel every morning between five and six; Masters were not to converse with Bachelors and Scholars except in chapel or hall; the College gate was not to be opened after half-past nine at night; all conversation in College was to be in Latin, &c. &c. The Fellows had to submit, and could only give vent to their feelings by expressing in the College Register their joy when the Visitation was over; an entry in November 6, 1641, notes that the Visitation, which had lasted three years and a half, and had threatened to rival the siege of Troy, was brought to an end by Divine Providence, "being the most unjust of Visitations, and worse than the worst of all."

In the Commonwealth time the whole University was for a brief period put under the power of very different Visitors—the Commissioners appointed by Parliament. Merton was itself a Puritan College, and numbered three of its Fellows among the Commissioners, while its Warden, Sir Nathanael Brent, was the President. These Commissioners and their successors practically governed the University from 1648 till Cromwell's death, and even Merton was during those years governed by them rather than by its own officers. Fellows and all other members of the College were summoned before them to make their submission, and those who refused were removed, though several of them were afterwards restored through Warden Brent's influence, and others regained their Fellowships at the Restoration.

After this date we hear little of complaints on the part of the College or vexatious interference on the part of the Visitor. Of late years he has continued to be the final Court of Appeal on questions touching the interpretation of the College Statutes and the like; when he has visited the College in person, he has appeared as a welcome and honoured guest, not as an inquisitor. Even the temptation to appoint his own chaplain as Warden is removed from him, since by the revised Statutes of 1881 the election of the Warden is now placed entirely in the hands of the Fellows.

We have said that the original foundation was for a "House of Scholars" (*Domus Scholarium* [1]), and that the modern distinction between Scholars and Fellows did not then exist; the only distinction was between the Scholar in his first year or probationary stage, and the same individual when finally elected. This being so, it is obvious that the junior members of the Society must have been in the majority, and we can well

[1] It should be remembered that "College" (*Collegium*) means the Society; "Merton College" strictly should mean the Warden and Fellows of Merton; the buildings in which such a Society lived would be called *Domus* or *Aula*. A survival of this correct method of designation may be found in the official term "Heads of Houses" and in the Christ Church men's custom of referring to their College buildings as "the House."

71

understand why such emphasis is laid in the Statutes upon the powers of the Senior Fellows. It is they who have to exercise discipline over the rest of the College, settle disputes, conduct elections, audit accounts, and manage the estates; and it is from them that the Deans and Sub-Warden are to be chosen. The Senior Fellows must have stood to the other members in much the same relation as the Warden and Tutors do to the undergraduates to-day.

The beginning of the undergraduate in the modern acceptation of the term, *i.e.* of students who joined the College but would not necessarily pass on to their Fellowships in due course, dates from more than a century after the foundation. John Wyllyot, Fellow of the College, Chancellor of the University in 1349, and afterwards Chancellor of the Diocese of Exeter, left funds in 1380 for the support of nine "poore schollers" who were to be called "Portionistæ" from their *portio* of commons; the name has somehow got corrupted into "Postmasters." It is clear that at first the "Portionistæ" were to be chosen young; they were to act as choir-boys in Chapel, wait on the Fellows in Hall, and live in a small house opposite the College gate, called "Postmasters' Hall"; so junior were they that a Bachelor Fellow, not one of the seven Seniors, was appointed to be their Principal and to watch over their behaviour and studies; they received assistance for a period of five years, and those who did well had hopes of succeeding in time to Fellowships ; when moved into College they at first had to share the rooms of the Senior Fellows. They did not reside in College till about 1575, when their number was increased to twelve ; subsequent benefactions have brought it up to twenty ; they have always had their own table in Hall. Postmasters' Hall, rebuilt in 1580, was afterwards the residence of the Wood family, and Antony Wood was born there (in 1632) and, except for the time when he had rooms in Merton College, lived the greater part of his life there.

Still the vast majority of Merton men now are neither Fellows nor Postmasters, but Commoners. The Postmasters came into existence more than a century after the Fellows, and the Commoners more than a century after the Postmasters. Four were admitted in 1497, but we are forced to the conclusion that they could not have been a success, as in 1566 the College refused to admit a Commoner even when recommended by the Earl of Leicester. It was not till the seventeenth century that they began to come continuously, though even then in quite small numbers ; and within living memory there were not more than fifteen or twenty. The Merton College of the past was therefore a small Society ; twenty to thirty Fellows, most of them clergymen, all celibate and living in College,

and thirty to forty Undergraduates, most
of them Postmasters or Bible-Clerks, and a
minority Commoners; these latter being
again divided into Noblemen, Gentlemen

ST. ALBAN HALL GATE

Commoners, and Commoners. A small
Society but a very cosy and pleasant one;
and we are glad to think that the traditions
of good fellowship formed when the College
was small have lasted on unimpaired to a

time when the total number of members is four times what it used to be, when the Undergraduates far outnumber the Fellows, and the Commoners far outnumber the Postmasters.

For Merton has not only grown within the limits of her own walls, but has absorbed the buildings and members of her next-door neighbour. In the absence of full records to illustrate the history of St. Alban Hall we have to collect what we can from the notes given us by Antony Wood and other antiquaries. It derives its name from a certain Robert of St. Alban's, a burgher of Oxford, who lived in the reigns of John and Henry III., and owned two houses which he bequeathed to the nuns of Littlemore, viz. St. Alban Hall which was on the east part of the present site, and Nun Hall upon the west. The latter was almost immediately after the foundation of Merton leased by the College as a house for the "Parvuli" or children of the Founder's kin, who by his Statutes were to be educated under the care of the Warden to the number of thirteen, and, when worthy, to be elected to Fellowships.[1] This lasted, according to Wood, till the reign of

[1] Fellows seem to have been elected pretty regularly on the ground of Founder's kin till the reign of Henry VII. (William Sheffylde was so elected in 1487); and nearly a century later (1577) Richard Fisher's father claimed a Fellowship for him on this ground; but the claim was disallowed and he was expressly elected on grounds of merit.

Henry IV., by which time there were no longer any applicants for the benefaction, and Nun Hall reverted to its earlier use. But the two Halls existed independently till about 1461, when they were united under the name of St. Alban Hall, and this was shortly afterwards leased to Merton College, who obtained the right of nominating one of their own Fellows as Principal. Possibly the Quad was then built by Warden Fitzjames. In the reign of Henry VIII. Wolsey obtained permission to dissolve the Littlemore nunnery and to employ its revenues for his new and magnificent foundation of Cardinal College. On Wolsey's downfall the King bestowed St. Alban Hall upon his physician, Dr. George Owen, who happened also to be a Fellow of Merton ; and the Hall, after passing through two or three hands, became in 1549 the property of the Warden and Fellows, but was some time after established as an independent academical Hall. It was finally restored to the College in 1882 on the retirement of its last Principal.

The members of the Hall were looked upon as being in some way connected with the College ; in 1626 we find provision made for them to have seats in the ante-chapel during service, and in 1639 they were directed by Archbishop Laud's Injunctions "to come into the Quire in Surplisses and Hoods." But the needs of one century are not quite the same as those of another, and there can be little doubt that in modern Oxford the smaller Halls, such as St. Alban Hall and New Inn Hall, did not meet any want that was not better provided for by the Colleges ; Merton did wisely, therefore, in annexing St. Alban Hall in 1882 ; since which time the buildings have become part of the College, and the Principal's house the residence (till 1904) of one of the College tutors.

The history of Merton College has not been marked by great or romantic crises ; bickerings between the Fellows, the Warden, and the Visitor, and conflicts with the City and the Townsmen, are features common to every College, and were inevitable in a mediæval University town. For more than a century after its foundation[1] it continued to be the leading College in Oxford, and it is at least probable that William of Wykeham gave to his own foundation the title of *New* College to distinguish it from Merton. The complaints both at Scrutiny and in Visitors' Injunctions of idleness on the part of the Fellows are more than counterbalanced by the famous names in Theology, Philosophy, and still more Medicine and Astronomy, that adorn the Merton Rolls right down to the sixteenth century.[2] In

[1] Henderson, p. 38.
[2] In Philosophy and Theology, Walter Burley and Thomas Bradwardine; in Medicine, John of Gaddesden, John Maudith, Simon Bredon; in Astronomy and Mathematics, John Ashynden, John Chambers, Sir Henry Savile ; see Henderson, pp. 39, 40, and Brodrick, *Memorials of Merton*, pp. 166 f., 173 f.

the fourteenth century many of the Fellows
favoured the Lollard Movement, and it is
possible though not certain that the
"Wyklyf" who was a Fellow in 1356 was
the great reformer; he may have been at
Merton before becoming Master of Balliol
in 1360.[1] In the early years of the next
century, however, Lollardism had been
completely banished not only from Merton
but from Oxford, by the vigorous action of
the Archbishops of Canterbury; but the
peace was not to be for long; Lollardism went
in the fifteenth century but the Reformation came in the sixteenth. It did not meet
with a welcome at Merton, which, contrary
to its sympathies both earlier and later, was
in Edward VI.'s reign strongly conservative.
Every one who loves an old Library and old
Manuscripts must sigh when he hears how
the Edwardine Visitors of 1550 conveyed
away a whole cartload of the Merton books,
not only theological but scientific, and how
these were burnt or given away or sold for
a mere nothing. This conduct may have
stiffened the Fellows in their opposition;
certainly they were prominent in welcom-
ing the Marian reaction, and we must
confess that when Latimer and Ridley were
burnt in 1555 both the acting Vice-
Chancellor (William Martial) who pre-
sided over the execution, and Richard
Smyth the Vice-Chancellor, who preached
the sermon, were Merton men. Things

See below, p. 90.

naturally changed with the accession of Elizabeth; some of the Fellows were expelled for refusing the Oath of Supremacy; with the advent of the John Mann mentioned above (p. 69) the College gained a strong Protestant Warden, and Archbishop Parker's Visitors expelled several more of the Fellows; and though Mann was Warden for but a few years, he was succeeded by an equally earnest and far abler Protestant, Thomas Bickley. During Bickley's reign and by his efforts[1] the College was completely cleared of sympathisers with Roman doctrine or practice.

During the latter part of Elizabeth's reign and for the whole part of James I.'s, Merton was ruled by Sir Henry Savile (1586–1622), and his Wardenship was probably the most brilliant epoch in the intellectual life of the College. Himself a fine classical and mathematical scholar and an untiring student, he took care both that reading men should be elected to Fellowships and that they should read when they were Fellows; during his reign many of the best-known scholars of the day were members of Merton, and one name is famous for ever not only at Oxford but over the whole learned world,—that of Sir Thomas Bodley, the founder of the

[1] No Probationer was admitted to his full Fellowship until he had renounced the errors of the Authority of the Pope, the Sacrifice of the Mass, Transubstantiation, and the Celibacy of the Clergy; see Henderson, p. 92.

Bodleian Library. Bodley was elected
Fellow in 1563, and set himself to his
great task in 1597; very possibly the
Merton Library and its delightful facili-
ties for quiet study may have been in his
mind, and have moved him to give all
members of the University the like privi-
leges on a larger scale.

With the reign of Charles I. a stormy
period set in. Popular as was the Laudian
ecclesiastical revival at Oxford, there were
two Colleges which were opposed to it,
Merton and Lincoln. The Warden, Sir
Nathanael Brent, was a Puritan, but had
of course to submit to Laud's Visitation
in 1638–41 (see above, p. 70). When,
however, war broke out between King and
Parliament, Brent sided with the latter,
and, on the approach of Charles to Oxford,
joined the Parliamentary forces in which
he exercised the office of Judge Marshal.
There was therefore no Warden to welcome
Queen Henrietta Maria when she came to
lodge in Merton (see above, p. 23), and
Charles may be excused under the circum-
stances for desiring to declare the Wardenship vacant and to place in it a loyal adherent
of his own. He had one for whom he was
anxious to provide in Dr. William Harvey,
his Court Physician, famous for all time
as the discoverer of the circulation of the
blood. He did not, however, openly order
the College to elect Harvey, but simply
directed the Fellows to present three persons,

for him to select one. Some of the Fellows
protested, and in the end eight names were
presented to the King; yet a majority of

THE QUEEN'S ROOM

the Senior Fellows placed Harvey first on
their list, and the King lost no time in
nominating him Warden. This was early
in 1645, and Harvey reigned at Merton for
only one year; in April 1646 the King

had to flee from Oxford, in June the City surrendered to Fairfax, Harvey retired to London, and Brent returned and resumed his Wardenship. In the College Register no account was taken of Harvey's year of office.

Brent, however, found the College denuded of its plate. Charles in 1643 had sent letters to all the Colleges and Halls demanding their plate to be melted down for his service at the Royal Mint set up in New Inn Hall; Merton contributed, according to Gutch, between 79 lbs. and 80 lbs., no doubt sorely against its will. The fine silver which may be seen in Hall and Common Room is all later than the civil war.

As we have seen above (p. 70), under the Commonwealth the College, or at any rate the larger Puritan majority in it, came to the front again. All the University was governed by the Parliamentary Commissioners, and Merton formed no exception; but as the Warden and several of the Fellows were members of the Commission, they could enjoy the luxury of regulating not only their own affairs but those of other Colleges as well. When the test question of submission to the authority of Parliament was put, Merton had fewer members expelled for refusing than any other College.

Yet we do not hear of deprivations or expulsions at the Restoration; lenient counsels prevailed with the external authorities, and very likely the College itself had had enough of Puritanism by that time and was ready to welcome the new régime. But fresh trouble was provided in the advent of an extremely unpopular Warden, Sir Thomas Clayton. We have a full account of him given us by Antony Wood, who collected with considerable care everything to his discredit. Even allowing for exaggerations, it is clear that Clayton must have been a man of poor parts and unamiable character, who tried to lord it over the Society just at the time when the Fellows were certain to resent anything that savoured of encroachment. He was nominated by the Visitor in 1661, but the majority of the Fellows were vehemently opposed to his appointment. On his arrival at Merton he found the doors locked and was unable to force an entrance into his lodgings; he had to assemble a band of followers and lay regular siege to the College, and it was nearly a month before the Fellows gave in and admitted him as their Warden. Nor was his tenure of office (and he was Warden thirty-two years) productive of happiness to himself or the College; there were constant bickerings and appeals to the Visitor. Wood's list of grievances is long and occasionally amusing. The furniture in the Warden's lodgings " being disliked by that proud woman (Lady Clayton) because, forsooth, the said goods were out of fashion, must all be chang'd

and alter'd to the great expence of the
College "; he burnt "in one yeare three
score pounds worth of the choicest billet
that could be had, not only in all his
roomes, but in the kitchin among his ser-
vants; without any regard had to cole,
which usually (to save charges) is burnt in
kitchins, and somtimes also in parlours ";[1]
he appropriated certain rooms in the Fellows'
Quad and made them part of the Warden's
house; he bought for his wife "a very
larg looking-glass, for her to see her ugly
face, and body to the middle "[2]; and so on.

Other excitements, equally distracting to
the College and to quiet study, though of
a pleasanter kind, were found in the visit
of Charles II. and his Court to Oxford.
In September 1665, when the plague was
raging in London, the King and Queen
arrived, Charles being accommodated at
Christ Church and Queen Katherine at
Merton; some of the Fellows were turned
out of their rooms to provide for the ladies
of the Court, and "ordinary prayers" were
said in Chapel (*i.e.* prayers in English) as
there were more women than scholars
there. The Queen and Court left in the
February following.

After Charles' death, Merton no more
figured prominently in big political move-

[1] Compare the note in the College Register, 14th
September 1640, that coal should be burned by way of
experiment instead of wood, the price of which had
greatly risen; see *Memorials of Merton*, p. 87.
[2] *Life and Times*, i. p. 396.

ments or was the scene of monarchs' sojourns either in the gloom of a civil war or in the careless gaiety of the Restoration; throughout the rest of the seventeenth and during the eighteenth century it was on the whole a Whig society, but living a quiet, comfortable, and possibly somewhat idle life. Warden Brodrick in his *Memorials of Merton* (p. 149) thus describes it : "In reviewing the College history between the Revolution and the accession of George III., we cannot fail to be struck by its comparative tameness. . . . Unlike All Souls, Merton was never seriously agitated by the fierce controversial spirit which prevailed both in London and Oxford under Queen Anne and the first Georges. . . . With the accession of George III., the history of Merton, like that of Oxford, gradually loses even its antiquarian interest, and glides placidly into the familiar stream of modern Academical life."

One more Royal guest lodged in Merton ; in June 1814 the Russian Emperor Alexander I. and his suite were lodged in Merton, and a large vase of Siberian jasper was presented by him in commemoration of the hospitality shown by the College. But in the nineteenth century the College has changed both outwardly and inwardly more than in any period of its history. Much of the fabric has been restored or altered, and Parliamentary Commissioners instituted first a set of Ordinances in 1857, and then a new code of Statutes in 1881 which have entirely superseded Walter of Merton's original regulations. None of the Fellows are now obliged to be either in Holy Orders or unmarried;[1] those who do not hold their posts as University Professors or College Tutors, can only be elected for a period of seven years, and are not bound to reside in College for more than one. The number of undergraduate members has multiplied, and a perpetual succession of examinations keeps the tutors always busy and no doubt keeps alive the diligence of their pupils; and through it all both tutors and pupils manage to have a very happy life. When at a College gaudy, Fellows and other old members of the College meet and talk over past years, no toast is greeted with warmer enthusiasm than

"Stet fortuna domus."

---

[1] Even in pre-Reformation times, many of the Fellows could never have taken orders; "medicus et uxoratus," or some similar description, is often recorded of them; they lost their Fellowships by marrying, but they could not have married at all if they had been priests: of Henry Brian (elected in 1455) it is said that he "afterwards took a wife, whom burying, he became a priest."
From Sir Henry Savile's time onwards (1585) the Wardens of Merton have as a rule been laymen; and until the last Oxford Commission Merton was the only College in Oxford where this was the case. Antony Wood speaks as if Sir Thomas Clayton were the first married Warden; but Savile married in 1592.

Patey's Quad

CHAPTER IV

NOTABLE MEMBERS OF MERTON COLLEGE

WE must begin this list with a few famous people who were not members of the College. The higher criticism has done its deadly work here as elsewhere, and forbids us now to claim names formerly accepted without question.

Duns Scotus, the famous scholastic philosopher and theologian, whose picture is in the Hall, could not have been a member of Merton, although the tradition which makes him so goes back to the fifteenth century. An entry in the old Catalogue gives a certain "Douns" (altered as it seems from "Doune") as scholar of the College during the reign of Edward II. (1307–27); and this has been supposed to mean Duns Scotus. But it seems practically certain that Duns Scotus had joined the Franciscan order by 1300 ; and in the face of Walter of Merton's Statutes he could neither have been elected to a Fellowship or retained one in 1307 or later ; the entry in the Catalogue must therefore refer to another person.

Roger Bacon has also been claimed for the College ; a certain "Bakon" is mentioned in the old Catalogue as a scholar in

the time of Edward I. (1272–1307), but the
name has been tampered with by a later
scribe and in its original form was much
longer, possibly " Bakeridge " or " Backn-
thorpe." And the same objection which
is fatal to Duns Scotus' claims also disposes
of Roger Bacon's; he must certainly have
been a Franciscan when the College was
founded, and so debarred by the Statutes
from membership.

With William of Ockham the case is
weaker still; his name does not appear in
the text of the old Catalogue but only in
the margin, and in a later hand. William
of Ockham too (who died *c.* 1349) was a
Franciscan, and so could not have been a
member; even Antony Wood doubted his
connection with the College.

On behalf of John Wyclif the reformer
(1324–84) there is much more to be said,
and Mr. Henderson [1] sums up in his favour.
It is certain that John Wyclif was Master
of Balliol in 1361; it is equally certain that
a " Wyklyf " was Fellow of Merton in 1356.
It is thus quite possible that the reformer
may have been a member of Balliol, have
left it after taking his M.A. degree (as many
Junior Masters did owing to the poverty of
the Hall), and then after being Fellow of
Merton for a short time, have rejoined his
old College, finally becoming Master. The
objection to the identification, however, lies

---

[1] *History of Merton College,* p. 291 ; see also art.
" Wycliffe " in the *Dict. Nat. Biogr.*

in the greater probability that the Merton Fellow was the John Wyclyve or Whitclyve who was appointed in 1361 to the Vicarage of Mayfield by Archbishop Islip (himself a Merton man), and to the Wardenship of Canterbury Hall in Oxford in 1365; and this Wyclyve was certainly a different man from the reformer. We cannot therefore do more than say that the reformer may have been a Fellow of Merton.

Turning to members whose connection with the College is unquestioned, Merton can claim two names really famous in scholastic philosophy and theology, Walter Burley and Thomas Bradwardine.

Walter Burley (1270 ?–1346) was a pupil but afterwards an opponent of Duns Scotus; he was a celebrated writer on philosophy, and bore the name of the *Doctor planus* or *Doctor perspicuus*. Like many early Mertonians, he afterwards obtained preferment in the Diocese of York.

Thomas Bradwardine (1290 ?–1349) was an even greater name in mediæval theology; he was known as the *Doctor profundus,* and was a mathematician, an astronomer, a moral philosopher, and a theologian. He must have entered the College some considerable time before 1323, when his name first appears on the College books, as then he was an M.A. of some standing. He was Proctor in 1325, and soon afterwards promotion and honours were showered on him. In 1337 he was Chancellor and Prebendary

of St. Paul's, Prebendary of Lincoln, and
Chaplain and Confessor to Edward III., ac-
companying that King to France; made
Archdeacon of Norwich in 1346, he was ap-

THE CHAPEL FROM THE EAST

pointed Archbishop of Canterbury in 1349,
but did not live to enjoy the Primacy long.
He was consecrated by Pope Clement VI.
at Avignon in the summer of 1349 and returned to England, but almost immediately

died of the Black Death (August 22). He
seems to have been a man not only of great
ability but also of noble life : in Theology
he stands out as one of the notable op-
ponents of the Pelagian tendencies which
were manifesting themselves in the later
Schoolmen, and his great work *De causa
Dei* is a strong vindication of the doctrine
of Predestination, on philosophical even
more than on theological or scriptural
grounds ; it was afterwards edited and published by Sir Henry Savile. Bradwardine
has the honour of being immortalised by
Chaucer in the " Nun's Priest's Tale "—

> " But I ne cannot boult it to the bren
> As can the holy doctour S. Austin
> Or Boece, or the Bishop Bradwirdyn."

In Reformation and post-Reformation
times we should remember :—

John Jewel (1522–71), Bishop of Salisbury, and famous apologist for the Church
of England, who was for a time member of
Merton. He entered in 1535, and was for
a short time Postmaster to John Parkhurst,
Fellow of the College, afterwards Bishop of
Norwich and one of the translators of the
Bible. Parkhurst trained Jewel well in the
study of Theology, and after four years
at Merton, Jewel was elected scholar, and
afterwards Fellow, of Corpus.

Of Sir Henry Savile (1550–1622) we have
spoken above (p. 79). Originally of Brase-
nose College, he was elected Fellow of

Merton in 1565, and was Proctor in 1575 and 1576; he was Reader in Greek to Queen Elizabeth, Provost of Eton in 1596, and was knighted by James I. in 1604. He was famous not only for his learning and accomplishments but also for his good looks; and was one of the most brilliant and successful Wardens that Merton has ever had. The Savilian Professorships of Geometry and Astronomy were founded by him.

Sir Thomas Bodley (1545–1613) was originally of Magdalen College, then Fellow of Merton; he was Proctor in 1569. Then, after being employed abroad on political and diplomatic business by Queen Elizabeth, he settled down again in Oxford and devoted himself to the task which has given his name more fame than any political successes would have done, the re-founding (1597) of the great University Library. Not only were books and MSS. collected, but he obtained in 1610 from the Stationers' Company the right for the Library to claim a copy of every book that should be entered at Stationers' Hall; it is this which as much as anything else has contributed to the value of the Bodleian Library. He died in London on January 28, 1613, and was buried with much pomp and honour in Merton College Chapel.

John Earle (1601 ?–1665), Bishop of Salisbury. He apparently matriculated at Christ Church, but was a B.A. and Fellow

JOHN EARLE, ANTONY WOOD

of Merton in 1621, was M.A. in 1624, and
Proctor 1631. He must have been a man
of charming manners and conversation, and
a most attractive character. Charles I.
made him tutor to Prince Charles, afterwards Charles II., who in turn made him
his Chaplain when they were abroad, and on
the Restoration made him successively Dean
of Westminster, Bishop of Worcester, and
finally Bishop of Salisbury. When the King
and Court came to Oxford in 1665, they
came from Salisbury, and Bishop Earle
seems to have accompanied them ; he was
lodged in University College, and was taken
ill and died there on November 17 ; he was
buried at Merton on the 25th, the funeral
being described at some length by Antony
Wood (*Life and Times*, ii. p. 66).

The life of Antony Wood (1632–1695)
has been described minutely by himself, and
his pages photograph not simply Merton but
the whole of the University at an extremely
interesting period ; he is no doubt often
bitter and not always accurate, but he is
always interesting, and the stores of information as to both past and present in his
books make them invaluable for the history
of Oxford. The fourth son of Thomas
Wood, he was born in December 1642 at
Postmasters' Hall, and educated partly at
New College School, partly at Lord
Williams' School at Thame. In October
1647 he was entered at Merton and
nominated Postmaster to Mr. Edward

Copley, a Fellow, and put into the chamber
under him in the great quadrangle. The
next Shrove Tuesday he had to bear his
part in the customary Undergraduates'
festivities in Hall; the freshmen were made
to stand on a form placed on the high
table and deliver mock heroic speeches;
according as they played their part well or
ill they were rewarded either with a cup
of "cawdle," or with salted drink and
"tucks," *i.e.* a method of torture which
consisted in applying a thumbnail to the
victim's chin in such a way as to make
the blood flow. Wood's speech, which
was rewarded with caudle, began : "Most
reverend Seniors, May it please your
Gravities to admit into your presence a
kitten of the Muses, and a meer frog of
Helicon to croak the cataracts of his
plumbeous cerebrosity before your sagacious
ingenuities," &c.; the rest that he has
preserved is harmless extravagant nonsense
enough. But in the following May he had
to undergo a far more serious trial before
the Parliamentary Commissioners who were
then in Oxford and were summoning all
the members of the University before them
and asking them whether they submitted
to their authority. Wood, whose sympathies were with the Royalists, answered
evasively, "I do not understand the business, and therefore I am not able to give a
direct answer ; " he would probably have
lost his Postmastership for this but for the

influence of the Warden, Sir Nathanael Brent, who was an old friend of his mother's.

Soon after (Nov. 1648), and through the same influence, his elder brother, Edward Wood, B.A. of Trinity, was made probationer-Fellow of Merton, and " being setled in the bay-tree chamber in the first quadrangle next to the gate of Merton Coll., A. Wood was put into the cockloft over him." In April 1650 Warden Brent made him a Bible-Clerk, the position being worth more than that of Postmaster; and he moved from the cockloft into the ground floor room in the "little or old quadrangle" (*i.e.* Mob Quad) opposite the Sacristy door. The next year his brother Edward was suspended for a time by the Parliamentary Visitors, partly on political grounds, and partly "for entertaining strangers at his chamber with more wine than 'twas thought convenient." Antony took his B.A. degree in 1652 and his M.A. in 1655, in which year his brother Edward died. About the same time the sight of a copy of Dugdale's *Warwickshire* fired him with the desire of attempting a similar work for Oxfordshire, and he devoted the rest of his life to antiquarian studies. His studies, however, did not improve his temper, and he had the unhappy art of quarrelling with most of his neighbours; he lived in College till 1673, when in consequence of a quarrel with the Fellows he went back to Postmasters' Hall, in which he had two little rooms fitted up for his work on the east side of the House. His life thenceforward was divided between researches into the history and antiquities of Oxford, music (of which he was passionately fond), and simple country walks and enjoyments with his friends; in spite of his quarrels he could write of the years following 1656: "What by music and rare books that he found in the public library, his life, at this time and after, was a perfect Elysium." Yet his tongue was so bitter that the Warden in 1677 told him he was "a disturber of the peace of the College," and when in 1680 he asked permission to examine the old College accounts, he was only granted permission provided he gave a promise "not to say anything prejudicial to the College." Wood died on the 29th of November 1695, and was buried in the ante-chapel, where Thomas Rowney, a personal friend, placed a monument to his memory.

Richard Steele (1672–1729) came up to Oxford in 1690 and matriculated at Christ Church, but in the next year was elected to a Postmastership at Merton. Here he was extremely popular, attained some reputation as a scholar, and wrote a comedy which, on the advice of a candid friend, he afterwards burned. Suddenly, in 1694, he left Merton without taking a degree, but " with the love of the whole Society," and entered the army as a gentleman-volunteer in the Life-Guards. He records how, when visiting Oxford some fifteen years later, "the sight of that College I am more particularly obliged to, filled my heart with unspeakable joy."

Shute Barrington (1734–1826), perhaps the most princely of all the Bishops of Durham, was educated at Eton, and afterwards entered as a gentleman-commoner at Merton. He took his B.A. degree in 1755, and obtained a Fellowship in the same or the following year. He was Chaplain to George III.; Canon of Christ Church, of St. Paul's, and of Windsor; Bishop of Llandaff in 1769, of Salisbury in 1782, and of Durham in 1791. He was a man of great wealth, but also of great generosity; a vigorous champion of the Protestant cause, he was opposed to the least political concessions being granted to Roman Catholics; yet at the time of the French Revolution he offered not only financial assistance but the utmost hospitality to the French emigrant Bishops and Clergy.

With the nineteenth century we are drawing near living memories and more familiar names; it would be superfluous to write biographies of members of the College who are or were personally known to Mertonians of the present day. But it may be interesting to note how few links serve to bind the Merton of to-day with what seems a distant past; the very year which saw the death of Bishop Barrington saw the election to the Wardenship of Robert Bullock Marsham, whose tenure

99

of office till 1881 (fifty-four years) con-
stitutes a record in the College History.
The last generation has indeed taken from
us many old members whose names were
famous in the political and ecclesiastical
history of the century; Cardinal Manning
was elected a Fellow in 1832, resigning his
Fellowship soon after on proceeding to a
benefice; Bishop Creighton entered the
College as Postmaster in 1862, and was
elected to a Fellowship in 1866; Lord
Randolph Churchill matriculated in 1867;
S. R. Gardiner the historian was elected
to a Fellowship in 1893; and the Hon.
George Charles Brodrick, most popular of
College Heads, kindest of friends, best of
hosts, most upright of men, was elected
Fellow in 1855, and was Warden from 1881
till 1903. But it is a more cheerful conclusion to such a handbook as this to be able to
point to those members of the College who,
famous in Church and State, in Science and
Literature, are still with us and we hope
may long be spared to us; to Lord Halsbury who entered the College in 1842; to
R. S. Copleston, Bishop of Calcutta, Postmaster in 1864; to J. W. Diggle, Bishop
of Carlisle, Postmaster in 1866; to E. A.
Knox, Bishop of Manchester, Fellow in
1868; to Andrew Lang, Fellow in 1868;
and to Professor E. Ray Lankester, Fellow
in 1891.

INDEX

INDEX

Common rooms, senior, 24, 60
Commoners, 73, 74
Commonwealth and Merton, 70, 82
Copleston, Bishop R. S., 100
Copley, Edw., 96
Creighton, Bishop, 100

"Dead Man's Walk," 63
Decanus, or Dean, 10
Diggle, Bishop J. W., 100
"Dormitory" theory with regard to the Library, 36
"Dove-cot," the, 29
Duns Scotus, 42, 89, 91
Durant, Warden, 53
Durham, William of, 1

Earle, Bishop, 94, 95
Edward I., 49
Edward II., 89
Edward III., 92
Edward VI., 78
Eighteenth century and Merton, 85
Elinor of Castile, 48
Elizabeth: Merton in her reign, 79
Elizabethan Prayer-book of 1560, 11
"Exchequer," the. See Treasury

Fellows, 8 n., 31, 51, 59, 64, 67, 70, 71, 75, 79, 82, 83, 86
Fellows, catalogues of, 33, 89, 90
Fellows' Garden, 28, 60, 61
Fellows' Quadrangle, 59
Fellows and Holy Orders, 67, 86
Fellows, senior, 10, 59 n., 69, 72, 73, 81
Fisher, A., 49
Fisher, R., 75 n.
Fitzjames, Warden, 27, 28, 40, 51, 54

Founder's kin, 9, 75
Founder's prayers, 11
Foxe, Bishop, 47
Franciscans, the, 89, 90
Front Quad, 14, 20

Gaddesden, John of, 77 n.
"Gallery," the, 25, 27
Gardiner, S. R., 100
Gargoyles on Chapel, 45
George III., 85, 99
Globes in the Library, 42
Grimwood, F. St. Clair, 53
Ground plan of Merton College, 21

Hakeborne, Richard de, brass of, 53
Hall, the, 22–24, 96
Hall, Mr. (Fellow of Merton), 69
Halsbury, Lord, 100
Harvey, Dr. William, 80–82
Henrietta Maria, Queen, 23, 80
Henry III., 5, 14
Henry IV., 76
Henry VIII., 76
Hodson, Christopher, 57

Ingram's Memorials of Oxford, 51 n.
"Injunctions" of Visitors, 64, 67, 69, 77
Islip, Archbishop, 91

Jacob the Jew, house of, 7, 31
James I., 79, 94
Jane, Dr., 68
Jewel, Bishop, 93

Katherine of Braganza, Queen, 84
Knox, Bishop E. A., 100
Kyllyngworth, John, brass of, 52

Lang, Andrew, 100
Lankester, Professor E. Ray, 100

102

INDEX

INDEX

Rodeborne, or Rudborn, Warden, 14
Rowney, Thomas, 98

SACRISTY, 23, 57, 58
St. Alban Hall, 7, 20, 28, 29, 61, 75, 76, 77
St. Frideswide's, Prior of, 7
St. John the Baptist, Church of, 7, 18, 54
St. Peter's in the East, 7
Savile, Sir Henry, 40, 53, 77 *n.*, 79, 86, 93, 94
"Scholars of Merton," 5-10, 71. *See also* Fellows
Scholastica, St., 49 *n.*
Scrutinies, 11, 67
Sever, Warden, 25, 27, 52, 58
Sheffylde, W., 75 *n.*
Ship-money, proclamation as to, 42
Shrove Tuesday festivities in Hall in Wood's time, 96
Site of College buildings acquired, 7
Skelton's prints of Merton College, 20, 24
Skipp, J., 50
Smyth, R., 78
Statutes, the, of 1264, 5
Statutes, the, of 1270, 7
Statutes, the, of 1274, 8 *f.*, 11
Statutes, the, of 1881, 86
Steele, Sir Richard, 98
Sub-Warden, the, 7, 10
Summer-house in garden, 25, 62, 63
Sun-dial on Chapel wall, 22
Sun-dial in Fellows' Garden, 62

TINTORETTO (?), picture by, in Chapel, 50

Tower of Chapel, 55
Tower of Chapel, cost of building of, 56
Transepts of Chapel, 45, 46
Treasury, the, 31-33
Trenge, Warden, 53, 68

UNIVERSITY College, 1

VASE of Siberian jasper given by the Emperor of Russia, 85
"Vestibule," the, 36
Vicenarius, the, 7, 10
Visitor, the, 10, 47, 64, 68, 69, 70, 71

WALTER of Merton. *See* Merton
Warden, the, 5, 8, 10, 71
Warden and Fellows, 68, 77, 83
Warden's garden, 61, 62
Warden's lodgings, 14, 19, 25, 26, 27, 59
Warham, Archbishop, 47
Watson, the Hon. E., 50
Whately, Archbishop, Principal of St. Alban Hall, 20
Whitgift, Archbishop, 39
Whytton, John, brass of, 52
Winchester, Bishop of, 64
Windebank, Col. Francis, 63
Window tracery in Chapel and Sacristy, 43, 44
Wolsey, Cardinal, 76
Wood, Antony, 17, 19, 25, 30, 51, 52, 53, 54, 56, 59, 62, 63, 69, 73, 75, 83, 84, 86, 95-98
Wood, Edward, 97
Wyatt's restorations at Merton, 23
Wyclif, John, 78, 90, 91
Wyllyot, John, 72

For EU product safety concerns, contact us at Calle de José Abascal, 56–1°,
28003 Madrid, Spain or eugpsr@cambridge.org.

www.ingramcontent.com/pod-product-compliance
Ingram Content Group UK Ltd.
Pitfield, Milton Keynes, MK11 3LW, UK
UKHW012337130625
459647UK00009B/354